MW01054504

Experiencing Theatre

Anne Fletcher
Southern Illinois University

Scott R. Irelan
Western Michigan University

focus an imprint of
Hackett Publishing Company, Inc.
Indianapolis/Cambridge

A Focus Book

focus an imprint of
Hackett Publishing Company

Copyright © 2015 by Hackett Publishing Company, Inc.

18 17 16 15   2 3 4 5 6 7 8

For further information, please address
    Hackett Publishing Company, Inc.
    P.O. Box 44937
    Indianapolis, Indiana 46244-0937

    www.hackettpublishing.com

Library of Congress Cataloging-in-Publication Data
Fletcher, Anne, 1953–
 Experiencing theatre / Anne Fletcher, Southern Illinois University ;
Scott R. Irelan, Youngstown State University.
   pages cm
 Includes bibliographical references and index.
 ISBN 978-1-58510-408-6 (pbk.)
 1. Theater—Study and teaching (Higher) 2. Theater—Production and
direction—Study and teaching (Higher) I. Irelan, Scott R. II. Title.
 PN2075.F55 2015
 792.02'32—dc22

                2015009504

Contents

PREFACE

Theatre in American colleges and universities is ubiquitous. It comprises programs in the thousands. It employs more scholars (and probably more practitioners) than any other kind of theatre. It introduces new generations to the experience of live performance and to an appreciation of theatre's place in the culture. It educates the many to understand what it means to be human, and it trains a few for a career in the art.

—Anne Fliotsos and Gail Medford, *Teaching Theatre Today: Pedagogical Views of Theatre in Higher Education*, ix.

To the Instructor

We write this book for three reasons. First, there appears to be a dearth of contemporary texts with a focused yet abbreviated look at the variety of job functions necessary to move a script from the page to the stage. Second, given the varied conversations we have had with colleagues from institutions in both the US and Canada, it is apparent that there are not many introductory texts available that offer a hands-on, activity-based approach that have been written with an open enough style, which encourages "doing" as a way of introducing learners to the art of live theatre. It is in the doing, the experiencing, that an appreciation of the art of theatre can and does emerge. Third, the existing books in this market are largely out of the price range for some, if not most, students enrolled in a one-semester foundation or appreciation course. In the end we offer this book as a way to prompt your own thinking about how to make learning visible, active, and experiential within any department regardless of size, financial resources, or curriculum goals.

In thinking about how to write *Experiencing Theatre* we sought ways to better activate material so that it opens both the eyes and ears of spectators to the aesthetics of experiencing live theatre. For many, this will be a new experience altogether. In fact, the audience to whom we address *Experiencing Theatre* is the learner who has never really seen live theatre. Keeping this in mind, our work augments the "job description" approach to introductory material with pertinent active-learning activities meant to provide a "flavor" of what theatre artists engage in daily. We rarely—and this is intentional—allude to particular plays. Our objective is to leave play selection to instructors who know their own classes, production seasons, and broader learning communities much better than anyone else. Several current introductory texts remain largely inaccessible to those who do not utilize their companion anthologies. We wish to avoid placing both instructors and students in a position where specific anthologies or single plays are necessary to follow the examples we discuss. While we choose not to take a theatre history approach to teaching introductory classes, often for non-majors, we hope that *Experiencing Theatre* might be coupled with another text to offer instructors who do incorporate more of the historical background a companion. We should also note that while we do offer several engagements, you may certainly elect not to do some of them, choose to devise your own, or even decide to ask learners to find ways to engage the material. In the end, our goal is to prompt your thinking as an instructor, not to dictate the rhythm of your course. If you are going to provide alternate engagements, then we suggest that you tell your learners so that they are not bogged down in reading material they will not be using. This is what we do in our own courses, and it has proven to be useful to developing a positive learning environment.

The pedagogy of *Experiencing Theatre* is grounded in both Howard Gardner's Theory of Multiple Intelligences and in notions of constructivist education, wherein learners take a more active role in building a core of knowing while acquiring applicable skills. Additionally, the course delivery this book encourages is that of active, experiential learning within a student-centered environment. We do this by structuring units of inquiry and exploration around primary concepts, posing problems to solve, and offering learning engagements that both seek and value learner perspectives on material. Practically speaking, this means we try our best to provide information and activities in a way that avoids the purely lecture/impart information paradigm, focusing, rather, on helping learners acquire pertinent terminology and key concepts, crafting activities that assist students in applying these terms and concepts, to construct an understanding of live theatre from where they are right now. In designing not only the units of inquiry but also the active-learning engagements we continue to ask ourselves how many different learning modalities we can involve to deliver the material in ways that prompt "doing" over merely memorizing. We hope you will, too, as you develop your own engagements in this manner. Lastly, while we do order the Explorations here, you can choose in what manner you would like to move through the material. We present them here in this order given the confines of publishing such a manuscript.

We wish to take this opportunity to thank all of our colleagues in ATHE, ASTR, and MATC who, over the past decade, have not only attended but also offered insights regarding the conference presentations of the material and ideas within this book. We also take this time to thank all of our collaborators at Focus Publishing for their work on this manuscript. We must also thank all of the graduate assistants who helped us clarify our ideas. They include Barry Berryhill, Randall Colburn, Laramie Dean, Kirsten Easton, Ken Ellis, Jessica Johnson Frohling, Michael Frohling, Anna Goller, Jaclyn Grogan, Whitney Johnson, Rick Jones, Patrick MacGregor, Jenny MacMurdo, John Robert Moss, Jonathan Myers, Guy Perticone, Nich Radcliffe, Vincent Rhomberg, Patrick Santoro, David Schneider, Courtney Self, John Ray Sheline, Aurora Strick, Shelley Stubbs, Nico Wood, Jenn Peterson, Casey Watkins, Becca Worley, Brooke Oehme, Matthew Wickey, Rory Leahy, Bobbi Masters, and Logan Reagan. SIU Department of Theatre Design/Tech Faculty Mark Varns, Dr. Ronald Naversen, Wendi Zea, and Bob Holcombe also had a large part in the development of material for the technical theatre aspects of *Experiencing Theatre*. A special thank you to Adam Parboosingh for his review of the scenography chapter, Fulton Burns for his contributions, Thomas Michael Campbell for all of his work, James Diemer for his keen eye and graphic skills over many iterations of this and our other work, Bevin Myake for her suggestions for the scenography chapter, and to Anthony Reed for creating some of the illustrations and contributing images and text representing his lighting designs.

For Further Exploration

Thomas Armstrong. *Multiple Intelligences in the Classroom,* 3rd edition (Alexandria, VA: Association for Supervision and Curriculum Development [ASCD], 2009). Print.

Jaqueline Grennon Brooks and Martin G. Brooks. *The Case for Constructivist Classrooms* (Alexandria, VA: Association for Supervision and Curriculum Development [ASCD], 1993). Print.

Howard Gardner. *Changing Minds: The Art and Science of Changing Our Own and Other People's Minds* (Boston, MA: Harvard Business School Press, 2004). Print.

——. *Five Minds for the Future* (Boston, MA: Harvard Business School Press, 2008). Print.

——. *Frames of Mind* (New York: Basic Books. 1985). Print.

——. *Intelligence Reframed: Multiple Intelligences and the 21st Century* (New York: Basic Books, 1999). Print.

——. *Leading Minds* (New York: Basic Books, 1995). Print.

——. *Truth, Beauty, and Goodness Reframed* (New York: Basic Books, 2011). Print.

Nancy Kindelan. *Artistic Literacy: Theatre Studies and a Contemporary Liberal Education* (New York: Palgrave Macmillan, 2012). Print.

Paul Woodruff. *The Necessity of Theatre: The Art of Watching and Being Watched* (New York: Oxford University Press, 2010). Print.

INTRODUCTION

There is no doubt that a theatre can be a very special place. It is like a magnifying glass, and also like a reducing lens. It is a small world, so it can easily be a pretty one. It is different from everyday life so it can easily be divorced from life.

—Peter Brook, *The Empty Space*, 98.

To the Student

Live theatre has always been surrounded by mystery and myths. Before we delve into the exercises, immersions, and discussions of *Experiencing Theatre*, we wish to address four common myths about working in the theatre.

MYTH #1: Live theatre is easy. Working in live theatre is hard, with long hours. Live productions often log over one hundred hours of rehearsal, not counting production meetings in which theatre personnel involved with the show work together toward achieving their vision of the production. While moving a text from the page to the stage is thrilling and gratifying, at the same time, we cannot deny that there are obstacles and frustrations along the route to production. In the end, problem-solving aspects of the process are often the most gratifying.

MYTH #2: No one can make a living by working in live theatre. Many people make a living in the field. As a matter of fact, both of us are writing this book thanks, in part, to the living we have made in live theatre. Regardless of whether someone dedicates himself or herself to a life in the theatre after further study, the skills gained from theatre study are invaluable to employers around the world. Who would not want an individual with the ability to think on their feet, speak confidently, reason logically, and collaborate freely?

MYTH #3: Most theatre people are crazy liberals with an agenda. Professionals in any field have a wide range of political and personal beliefs. Live theatre is no different. For example, writer David Mamet and Steppenwolf company member Gary Sinise are both politically conservative, the latter being the founder of "Friends of Abe," while others like Barbara Streisand and Whoopi Goldberg frequently speak out on definitively politically liberal points of view. Theatre is no different from any other field in that its personnel include people of a wide range of beliefs, political or otherwise.

MYTH #4: Live theatre events are going by the wayside due to technological advances and cuts in funding. Though demographics change and attendance numbers ebb and flow, up-and-coming generations still hold a special place for live performance events. New technologies are being integrated into live performance, and several new books address this phenomenon. We write *Experiencing Theatre* for future spectators—for you, the next generation of audiences.

Some Basic Principles of Live Theatre

Theatre is interdisciplinary, collaborative, and global. By this we mean that, first, live theatre always incorporates study and application of information and skills from other fields. Directors utilize principles from music, like rhythm and tempo, as they move performers across the stage. Comedies typically have a faster pace than tragedies or serious dramas. Designers study visual art, architecture, art history, and engineering so they have a wealth of styles and techniques from which to draw as they go about their work. Writers (or group collaborators) probe different subject areas as they gather research material for compiling their scripts or performance texts. Current events become important for politically or socially active theatre companies. Theatre is collaborative. While there is a **genre** (meaning type or kind) of theatre devoted to **solo performance** (one-person), even then, it is likely that at the site of the production someone other than the performer will design or at least operate the lights and run the sound. Many artist/practitioners contribute to the production process—writers, directors, designers, etc.—and work together to create a final product. It is the final product that is imperative as paying patrons eventually arrive to engage in watching. For this reason many of the exercises in this book are group activities. Lastly, our society is global, meaning that geographic and social borders blur. Live theatre today must address global issues of concern to remain vital through production techniques that represent approaches from many locations and cultures.

How to Use this Book

Experiencing Theatre is created primarily for use in introduction to theatre classes as a way for learners to enter the world of theatrical production. This said, it can be explored outside of the formal classroom too by anyone interested in watching live theatre. The text is designed in an activity-based style, full of exercises, complete with explanations of types of plays and performances, design elements, production values, theatre spaces, audience outreach techniques, job descriptions of roles in the theatre, and the like. Our goal is to take the reader through the experience of both accomplishing tasks and using skills that live theatre practitioners execute and utilize in their daily work of conception, collaboration, and creation. Your instructor may supplement *Experiencing Theatre* with plays to read, productions to view, writing exercises to complete, and other activities as you explore the exercises we provide. In the end, whether you are a theatre major/minor or someone who is looking for a general education regarding the art of live theatre, *Experiencing Theatre* asks you to stretch beyond your current appreciation of theatre as an art form by doing a variety of production-based activities.

We all learn differently. Exercises in this book are designed to appeal not only to those who enjoy writing, drawing, speaking, and researching but also to those of you who may like the highly physical work that comes with either acting or directing. We believe that we all remember key concepts and terms by experiencing them—by not only reading and studying but also by doing. That is, if as learners we can experience something or somehow "get it into our body," then we will come to appreciate it better. By doing so, then, we can value the work of others in new ways. When we attend a live performance, then, we can fully respect the range of both talent and hard work that went into creating the production.

We also feel that although this may be challenging or even frightening, we all need to "jump right in" sometimes, and debrief our experience later. For this reason each chapter begins with what we call an "Immersion." You do not need to know anything about the information in the upcoming section to experience the Immersion. Just do it! "Exercises" are placed throughout each chapter, interspersed with explanations, definitions, and examples, as a way to further encourage experiences with the material at hand. This pattern continues across the book: Jump in with an Immersion. Read, study, do. Complete more exercises. Review.

For Further Exploration

Anthony B. Dawson. *Watching Shakespeare: A Playgoers' Guide* (New York: St. Martin's Press, 1988). Print.

Ken McCoy. *A Brief Guide to Internet Resources in Theatre and Performance Studies*. 11 September 2014. Web.

John O'Toole, Madonna Stinson, and Tina Moore. *Drama and Curriculum: A Giant at the Door* (Netherlands: Springer Media E-Book, 2009). 29 September 2014. Web.

EXPLORATION ONE

What Is Theatre?

There is an art to watching and being watched, and that is one of the few arts on which all human living depends. If we are unwatched we diminish, and we cannot be entirely as we wish to be. If we never stop to watch, we will know only how it feels to be us, never how it might feel to be another.

—Paul Woodruff, *The Necessity of Theatre*, 10.

IMMERSION #1
What is theatre? What is live performance?

1. From your own personal experience, what do you think theatre and live performance "is"? Write your answer in approximately two or three sentences.
2. In groups of no more than five, make a list of everything you think needs to be present for theatre to occur. Start here:

   Watchers or Audience

3. Refine the list together. See if you can group the items under SPACE, PERFORMER(S), WATCHER(S), and IDEA(S). These four components have long been necessary for theatre to happen.

Theatre

Definitions of theatre vary greatly. Dictionaries often list first the use of the word as it pertains to the building in which plays and other performance events are presented, rather than focusing on the experience of theatre. Many authors and educators emphasize plays as written when they attempt to define theatre, ignoring its "liveness" with bodies on stage communicating to persons watching. Some books, like this one, discuss elements of theatre instead of becoming wed to a single, all-encompassing definition. We like the way theatre scholar Tracy C. Davis and others define theatre as **"an art concerned almost exclusively with live performances in which the action is precisely planned to create a coherent and significant sense of drama."** This definition reinforces the idea that theatre involves live bodies—some onstage, some offstage, and at least one in the audience—and that the experience is somehow ordered. By using the words "sense of drama" Davis (and other authors) imply some sort of emotional reaction or at least increased awareness on the part of spectators, if not the participants as well. We like this definition because it remains open-minded and allows us to include many kinds of productions and processes in our discussion of theatre.

Sets, costumes, and lighting—along with what we call performative qualities like actor/participants, dialogue, and maybe even song(s)—are all recognizable elements of theatre. These alone, though, are missing one major element generally associated with live theatre—a written script. While we need to keep an open mind as to what constitutes theatre, we must also recognize the purpose of particular events and differentiate between traditional, scripted plays and devised (or ensemble) pieces that are often crafted by groups. We also need to think about the purpose of the event, its efficacy, and how that might further delineate it from live theatre—what we often refer to as live performance. Why is the event being held? Is it to celebrate a marriage or other special occasion? Is it to rally voters for a particular candidate? Is it a competition or a sporting event? All of these events have performative qualities, but not everyone would consider them theatre. Storytelling, myth, and ritual, and variations thereof, are types of live performance that utilize theatrical elements but do not necessarily result in a "written blueprint" for live theatre or what we refer to as a **playscript**. It is this written blueprint, no matter how loosely constructed, that distinguishes live theatre events from those that are simply live performance events.

Live Performance

There are many events that happen in the moment, which require interaction with at least one watcher. We define these as **live performance**. For example, a rock concert might be considered live performance because the performers and spectators are together in the present moment, interacting with one another, creating the once-in-a-lifetime experience. The concert may even sequence songs so that the sets tell a story. Some concerts might be thought of as theatre because the songs themselves offer a script of sorts but are still without a plot. On the other hand, in experiencing film, for example, a watcher is engaged in the present, but the film was created elsewhere and at a different time, so there is no sense of liveness involved. Therefore a film is not live performance.

We should view live theatre, then, as any performance event that has four basic elements: **Space**, **Performer(s)**, **Watcher(s)**, and

Exercise #1
Live Theatre or Not?

Instructions: *Read the following descriptions, and, with no further knowledge but your personal experience and the ideas about theatre you discussed in Immersion #1, determine whether each illustrates theatre.*

1. We are in Taiwan and people are parading through the streets. Other people line the streets, watching. There are dancers wearing face paint and white, bifurcated, big toe socks. There are little cars that look like Volkswagons covered by big foam carvings that have what appear to be signs of the zodiac on them. We all arrive at a tent. It is practically filled with flowers, especially lotus blossoms. There is a lot of fruit too. There is a picture of a man. The music stops. Is this experience theatre?

2. We are on a street in a busy city square. In front of a coffee shop we see a man sitting on the sidewalk, typing on an old-fashioned manual typewriter. He has a hat for contributions sitting in front of him, and a sign encouraging anyone who wants to type to do so whenever they feel moved. From time to time he turns to his right and stacks/unstacks coffee cups that are arranged in a tower formation. Is this experience theatre?

3. A wingwalker walks on the wing of an airplane while it is in flight. Is this experience theatre?

4. A van of football fanatics travels to watch the Iowa Hawkeyes take on the Ohio State Buckeyes. They have purchased tickets in advance. Once there, they unpack and begin tailgaiting. As game time approaches they make their way into the stadium. They have seats in the end zone. They watch the game. Is this experience theatre?

Idea(s). That is, for us theatre is live and in the moment, complete with both watcher(s) and performer(s) sharing the same space and time. We believe that theatre is in some way ordered or structured around ideas. That order may stem from a formal script or from some other type of written component such as an outline or storyboard. Such is the case with performance by professional groups whose live performance pieces clearly tell a story, though the elements seen are not always fully scripted. What we argue for here, then, is a broad definition of theatre.

As a way to further our understanding of live theatre and how to define it, let us revisit something from our early years of schooling—reading aloud. Reading a story aloud illustrates storytelling. A single person reading the story aloud with minimal actions, or even telling the story from memory, would still constitute storytelling (live performance). When adding performative qualities, like embodying characters, the activity of reading moves into the realm of live theatre. This is how historians believe the ancient Greeks progressed from the ritual of recounting their tales through song to embodying what happened when humans betrayed the mandates of the Gods. A formally organized and more polished performance of the embodied tale eventually found its way into particular forms of drama and production at a variety of theatrical festivals (i.e. City Dionysia). Accordingly then, on some level, contemporary live theatre has its roots in ancient ritual activity. For our purposes here, we define **ritual** as behaviors or actions performed at least twice, for the same purpose. While we use the word ritual in speaking of daily activities, like brushing our teeth, what we mean here has more of a spiritual, ceremonial, or social purpose. So, is brushing your teeth a ritual? No. It is simply ritual behavior because there is no spiritual or ceremonial purpose. We have all heard, for example, of particular harvest rituals in which particular indigenous groups employ song, dance, and maybe some sort of prayer in the hope of achieving a good crop. This is ritual. Christian religious services are imbued with rituals particular to spiritual principles of a given denomination.

We offer the following three exercises to help clarify differences, similarities, and overlaps between theatre and other performances with which you might be already familiar. Whether you do these exercises as part of a formal learning session or not, review them carefully and reflect on what you are being asked to consider.

In thinking about storytelling and ritual in relationship to live theatre, we can begin to appreciate how live theatre incorporates or at least embraces aspects of storytelling and ritual. The ancient Greeks were well aware of this confluence. We move on now to consider six major elements of theatre. As we do this, remember that live theatre at its most basic requires Space, Performer(s), Watcher(s), and Idea(s).

Exercise #2
Storytelling and Performance

Instructions: *This exercise begins with someone reading aloud the story "Little Red Riding Hood" (or another familiar piece). Next, form groups of no more than six.*

1. Find a space and sit in a circle on the floor.
2. Someone gets in the middle and starts reading "Little Red Riding Hood" (or another familiar piece) to the rest.
3. Shortly into the story, the reader uses his or her voice and maybe movement to "act out" the story.
4. Someone else jumps into the center of the circle and assumes one of the other roles.
5. Someone else jumps into the circle and takes on a third role.
6. Work together to create a refrain for those in the circle to read/perform.
7. Add characters as desired.
8. Solidify as a short performance.

Exercise #3
Ritual and Performance

Instructions: *Divide into groups of no more than six. Create and then perform a short ritual based on "Little Red Riding Hood" (or another familiar tale). Your ritual must include:*

► Movement in unison.

► Movement in smaller groups, trio, pair, etc.

► Repeated movement or activity for a particular purpose/desired end result.

► Minimum "lines" or dialogue, but it may include a spoken "refrain" or "chorus."

Exercise #4
Storytelling, Ritual, and Live Theatre

Instructions: *Get into groups of four or five max. Designate a person to read the story "Little Red Riding Hood" (or another familiar piece) to the group. Each group will re-imagine a "treatment" of the story according to the directions below. Groups will create "A," "B," or "C" versions.*

"A" Version	"B" Version	"C" Version
Find a way to retell the story as an explanation or as the origin/ creation of something. Write nothing down. Just tell the story.	Tell the story including words or activities repeated exactly the same way at least three times, and for the same purpose, desire, or outcome.	Make a list of performative elements (and describe them) that could be used to stage the story and the repeated words/activities from "B."
(Storytelling)	(Ritual)	(Theatre)

Elements of Theatre

In the fourth century BCE, Greek writer Aristotle produced a guide to play analysis known as *The Poetics*. Much like a scientist trying to classify species of plants and animals, he offered six elements of a successful drama. We introduce Aristotle's six elements here because they are a useful place to begin thinking about plays on the page (**form**) versus plays on the stage (**style**). We also use these elements because, to some extent, contemporary ways of analyzing plays either stem from or work against Aristotle's elements of plot, character, idea, language, music, and spectacle.

Plot is an ordered sequence of events. This differs from **story**, which is an entire narrative of related incidents from which the writer

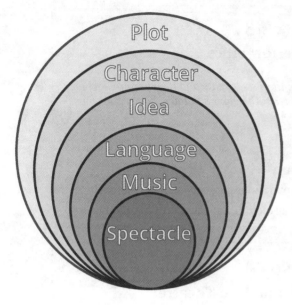

Fig. 1-1— Aristotle's Six Elements.

selects the plot. Plot often condenses and gives some sort of coherence to an extended, winding story. Have you ever been bored by a friend's long description of a movie? This is because s/he was telling you the whole story. Plot can be boiled down to specific events, strategically arranged by the playwright. It has been said that a playwright never writes about a day in which nothing much happens. Remember that the playwright crafts the events in the piece and heightens the action. What would happen if you removed the murderer from a murder mystery story? The plot would be changed, and the action could not continue. Plot is the most important element of drama as it surrounds all other elements. If something is weak in the plot, then that weakness will spread across all other elements.

Character refers to the person(s) created to carry out actions of the plot in ways that, to some extent, imitate elements of daily, lived experiences. This is one of the easiest Aristotelian elements to identify with because we are in contact with humans and human behavior on a regular basis. As compelling as dramatic characters may be, you should always keep in mind that they serve as a function of the plot. Each character plays his or her part in conveying the story. That is, a writer has crafted them as part of the overall blueprint. We have all seen films or television shows in which we recognize the villain and his/her function in the plot. If we remove the murderer from a murder mystery, then we have lost an important character, and the plot is ruined.

Idea (or thought) refers to meaning(s), message(s), or thematic concern(s) that are part of the written text.

Language is the primary tool writers use to put across the idea(s). Language not only takes into account the literary quality of a text—tone, mood, rhyme, imagery, allusion, and the like—but also encompasses lines and the way they are spoken during a live performance. So, a British accent, for example, falls into the category of language. This element is much more relevant to watching rather than reading a piece of theatre.

Music, as Aristotle wrote about it, referred not only to the singing of choral odes and dialogue in Greek Tragedy but also to its instrumental accompaniment. For the contemporary watcher, music relates not

Exercise #5
Aristotelian Collage

This exercise asks you to look at contemporary media and its use of these elements to tell a story, usually the story of a product.

Keeping in mind Aristotle's six elements (plot, character, idea, language, music, spectacle), skim through magazines and gather images and words that you will arrange into a collage. The collage should contain an image of a character, and at least one other image to represent another force or character that pushes back against the first—at least two opposing characters. Also include images that indicate "spectacle"—visual production elements (costume, set, lights) providing the "stage" for your story. (These do NOT have to be literal, merely suggestive. They may be splashes of color, inspirational images that evoke mood or texture.) As you arrange your collage, formulate a central idea or theme that your story will convey to the audience: "love conquers all," "war is bad," "the apple doesn't fall far from the tree," etc.

When you've finished your collage, make a list of one-sentence descriptions of:

- ▶ The plot (this is the story of …)
- ▶ A brief description of the opposing characters
- ▶ The idea(s) conveyed
- ▶ One sample line of dialogue that will help convey the idea
- ▶ A brief description of the requirements for the spectacle (Where does the story take place? What sorts of costumes? What sorts of lights?)

---

only to actual music tracks (underscoring), accompaniment or singing in a musical theatre production, or opera with live band or orchestra, but also to the musical qualities of language—pitch, rhythm, tone, intonation, and the like. This element is much more relevant to watching rather than reading a piece of theatre.

Spectacle or "something seen" includes all the visual elements in a production—costumes, scenery, lighting, etc. In reading, all references to these elements in **dialogue** (spoken lines) or in written stage directions indicate what is to be seen. For example, Character A says, "Look at that shiny star" and a burst of light pops up somewhere on stage. This element is much more relevant to watching rather than reading a piece of theatre.

Ultimately, Aristotle's elements work together in various combinations. Some playscripts may be called "character-driven." This is when characters are of primary importance to the action of the plot. Others might be referred to as plot-driven. This is when what happens and in what order is most important to your experience. Although sometimes the idea comes from within the text (**intrinsic idea/meaning**) and

Fig. 1-2— SIU Theatre 101 Students Working on Storytelling and Performance

sometimes it comes from the culture in which it is being produced (**extrinsic idea/meaning**), idea is always present. Again, these elements work together as we encounter a piece on the page for the first time. These elements, too, drive artistic choices as we move from page to stage.

We now consider why Aristotle's first three elements are extremely helpful in examining the "blueprint" as written. In doing so we point to the tools needed to appreciate dramatic literature on the page. While live theatre, television, and film all share common storytelling elements, they are radically different modes of delivery. Because many of you are probably more familiar with film and television, though, we use language that encompasses all three modes of delivery. While we emphasize Aristotle's elements in groups of three, it is important to remember that they are interrelated and each has influence on the other elements.

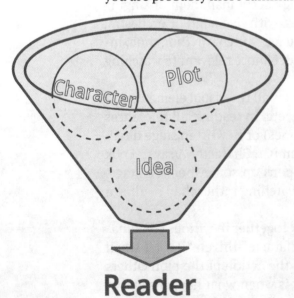

Fig. 1-3—Plot, Character, Idea, Reader

Reading a Play

As suggested, reading a play and seeing one in live performance are two distinct experiences. Reading is concerned solely with literary aspects of what is written, whereas seeing focuses on how literary aspects can activate watcher interest (and even participation). As suggested, the script offers a

Play	Prose
Speaks from author to audience through an intermediary group of persons, largely through first-person "voice"	Speaks from author to audience directly, largely through third-person "voice"
Incomplete experience without performance in front of watchers	Experience is complete and done in isolation
No narrative voice telling what to see and think	Narrative voice dictates aspects of the story at hand
Large amounts of information left out	All details provided
Names of characters appear above/beside words to be spoken and action to be completed	Character names and actions are integrated seamlessly

Fig. 1-4—Differences in Reading Experiences

blueprint for what will become the live performance event. A writer crafts what will happen and how that happening will unfold. In both modern and contemporary Western theatre, this means that some sort of printed text provides the architecture to build an imagined world. Readers experience this world largely through **stage directions** (directions in a published script printed in italics).

Readers also experience the world of the play by following character motives and how they carry out those motives, which are often revealed through character dialogue. Like any blueprint, however, this is only a partial view of a final product. That is, without the immediacy of interaction between the watcher and the stage—liveness—reading is an incomplete theatre experience. Put another way, while reading a script is often fulfilling, it is unfinished theatre because it has not received the input of many other collaborators—including directors, designers, performers, and, perhaps most importantly, watchers.

While the writer may describe what the world of the play looks like, scripts do not always allow for the extensively detailed explanations of the complete theatrical environment in ways a novel or short story might. Even in contemporary dramas the "Who," "What," and "Where"

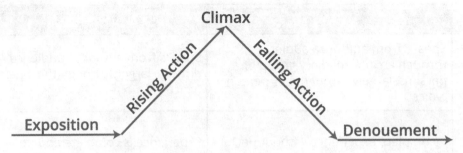

Fig. 1-5—Linear/Cause-and-Effect/Causal Plot Structure.

of theatre comes from experiencing characters in action and design elements in real time, not just from following the words on the page. Therefore, the reading experience remains two-dimensional until a creative-collaborative team comes together and builds a three-dimensional production based on a given blueprint. In order for this to happen, each member of a **production team** (the group of people mounting the play on the stage) must read and reread the script for clues to how they might construct a unified production, one where all the elements work together to put across a single, agreed-upon vision of what watchers will experience. So, our approach to reading a play here will be centered on that of team members looking for information that would help us to mount the production. Given this, we will now focus on acts of analysis because every member of the production team finds his/her inspiration for artistic choices from encounters with the script in its written form.

Following Aristotle's lead, we start play analysis with plot. There are two broad categories you can use when thinking about plot. **Linear plot**, also referred to as a cause-and-effect or causal plot, is one in which a particular event leads to another: A-B-C-D—Z. Without the happenings and information in A there can be no B and so on with C, etc. Linear plot structures can be subdivided into two types: those of a single-line plot and a multi-line plot. The former is just that, a plot with only one line of action to follow, while the latter has more than one line of action (subplots) to follow until all of them converge. An **episodic plot**, also referred to as a non-linear or mosaic plot, is one where incidents do not necessarily follow each other because of

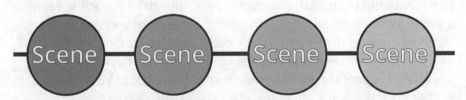

Fig. 1-6—Episodic/Vignette Structure

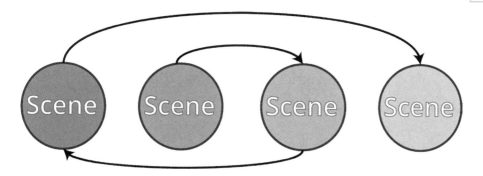

Fig. 1-7—Non-Linear Structure

a previous event but rather are guided by an overarching idea or thematic concern(s).

Shakespeare's plays offer wonderful examples of how two or three concurrent plots work within a multi-linear, episodic structure. Many contemporary texts may appear to have no plot at all when first read. However, further analysis often reveals a carefully constructed sequence of events. Each of these broad plot structures has several components to look for as you read.

One of the first plot elements to note is **point of attack** (aka POA), the place in the story where we enter the world and the plot begins to unravel before us. There can be a late point of attack or an early point of attack. A **late point of attack** is when the plot starts late in the story as opposed to an **early point of attack**, which starts early in the story. A play with a late POA often includes a lot of **exposition** or background material regarding what happened previous to our "arrival" in the plot. This is because so much of the story has happened before we join the world of the characters that we need to be caught up. When dealing with an early POA, you will find yourself spending much more time with characters and much less time reading the deliberate revealing of background information. Closely related to this are conflict, complication, and the crisis moment. **Conflict** is when a character or force stands in the way of another character and **complication** is when a desired outcome is blocked by another character or force. There may be a series of complications within a play that eventually leads to the **crisis moment**, which is when the

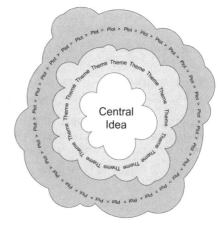

Fig. 1-8—Mosaic Plot Structure
(Diagram courtesy of Anthony Reed)

Exercise #6
Characteristics of the Linear Plot

To be completed in pairs or small groups.

Instructions: *Review the previous diagram that illustrates linear (or causal) plot structure. Review a well-known short story of your choice. Identify the component parts of the story and then arrange them as a linear plot. If you want to, draw a diagram and list the moments in the story that correspond to each part.*

▶ What conflict(s) are apparent in the story?

▶ What background information is revealed? Is the background information presented in description(s) or in dialogue or both?

▶ What are the story's given circumstances (education, economic status, geographic locale, and other conditions)?

▶ How did one event in the story lead to the next?

▶ What is the high point of the story's action? The point from which a character cannot return?

▶ How does the story "wrap up"?

Exercise #7
Episodic/Mosaic Plot

To be completed in pairs or small groups.

Instructions: *This time you will take apart the well-known story of your choice and reassemble it in episodic or mosaic structure.*

1. Once again, look at the major actions of the story. List them in order. Leave enough space on the page between items in the list to cut them out.

2. Note repeated actions, images, or ideas.

3. Cut the items on your list into strips of paper.

4. Organize the strips of paper (the story's major actions) into groups that somehow go together (character, repeated words, images, ideas). If possible, then identify a central idea around which you can organize the actions.

5. Read aloud what you have noted on the strips of paper, in the new order.

You have constructed an episodic or mosaic plot structure.

lead character realizes they have made choices from which they can never return. From this point forward, the rest of the plot must logically lead to a wrapping up or conclusion (**resolution**). Although locating these specific plot elements is often much easier in a linear plot, to some extent, they are present in a non-linear plot as well. In fact, some mosaic plot structures might resemble linear plots in that their action steadily progresses, eventually drawing to a conclusion from the convergence of different actions, with similar thematic concerns. Plays comprised of a series of short scenes, vignettes related in some way, often reflect this structure.

As previously mentioned, while both television and film lack liveness, they often provide us with opportunities to review what we learn about live theatre. As you attend movies or watch television programs in the coming days, notice how their plots are arranged.

Character

There have been many kinds of characters over the course of time. Thankfully we can distill them down into the following broad categories. The lead character, also referred to as the **protagonist**, is the most important person with regard to the plot. The **antagonist** stands in opposition to the lead character. A **confidant(e)** character is one that supports a main character, either the protagonist or the antagonist, and offers them a chance to speak their mind in ways that allow us to gain important information that may be kept secret from other characters. Think of the confidant(e) as a "best friend." Historically, Shakespeare uses confidant(e) characters quite well. Look for nurses attending to young ladies or young men speaking with priests in plays like *Romeo and Juliet* for good examples. The **foil** sets off another character through contrast—funny to dull, smart to dim-witted, sexy to dumpy. As in prose fiction, characters can be credible or not. They can also be sympathetic or not. Sometimes a writer literally gives voice to his or her thoughts through the **raisonneur** character. The writer might also elect to use a **narrator** character as a way to offer insight into past events or as a way to guide us through the story of the play. A play from history that we find quite helpful in reviewing when thinking of a strong narrator character is Thornton Wilder's *Our Town*.

Writers leave many clues to character in their texts. Two of the best places to look for these clues are the cast of characters list at the beginning of the play and the stage directions. While you may not find out much in terms of deep motivation, you should be able to come away with basic life information (education, economic status, geographic

Exercise #8
Character

Large or small group discussion (may be completed individually).

Instructions: *Using a well-known fairy tale or myth, identify what kinds of characters are present in the story being told.*

- ▶ Who is the lead character, the one who is trying to achieve something (protagonist)?
- ▶ Who is the force working against the main character (antagonist)?
- ▶ Is there a foil? A confidant(e)?
- ▶ If you read the original story aloud, then how does the narrator function?
- ▶ Does the person reading the story represent the author's point of view?
- ▶ Is the reader a raisonneur?
- ▶ Is a character within the story's action a raisonneur?

locale, and other conditions). Two other places to look are in the lines characters speak about themselves and the lines spoken about them by others. Just as in daily life, though, these can be less reliable sources based on the motives of the character speaking the lines. If a character is a braggart, then maybe everything s/he says about life is exaggerated. If a character is battling with dementia and/or substance abuse, then his/her perspective might be skewed by his/her altered perception of reality. Whatever the case might be, you should always look to what characters do since actions do indeed speak louder than words. In the end, as in "real life," how a character relates to those around them can help you learn more about who they are and how they function in their world.

Idea

Idea, or a message being communicated, is paramount in both reading and seeing a play. While practitioners working on the same script may not agree on only one main message, they can usually identify similar theme(s), sometimes focusing primarily on one. It is also from this consideration of theme that a **concept** often emerges. In this case a concept is the metaphorical or imagistic expression of ideas a written text inspires. The saying "The concept (car) drives the theme" is a helpful way for you to differentiate between the two. Put another way, an overall idea (concept) helps to visually communicate the theme(s) or message(s) in production.

Exercise #9
Idea, Theme, and Concept

Large or small group discussion (may be completed individually).

Instructions: *Recall how episodic or mosaic plot structure requires an organizing principle, a rationale for where to place each of the strips of paper used in Exercise 7 with the story's actions written on them. Now, think about the story in more abstract terms.*

▸ What are the story's main ideas?

▸ What message(s) or theme(s) is the story trying to put forth?

▸ Do we learn a lesson from the story?

The way the production looks, feels, sounds, etc. is based on both literary analysis and artistic interpretation. For example, you see live theatre that is about a tangled web of lies, which underscores how falsehoods ultimately get us in trouble and result in our downfall (theme). A director uses ropes and knots as an image to view the "strands" of the script as a spider web (concept). The production ends up with strands of rope hanging from the ceiling that are manipulated by the characters when they enter and exit. How did the production team arrive at these decisions about style? Just as we do in Exercise 11, they read the play—multiple times—and looked for, among other features, repeated images.

Answering these questions will lead you to discovering possible themes and concepts. When we apply these questions to plays, we are on the road to determining how the production might look onstage.

Before moving on, we must pause and spend a little more time on two broad ways that a play can look on the page and then on the stage.

Realism and Non-Realism

Regarding both form (play on the page) and style (play on the stage) it is helpful to consider two broad categories: **Realism** and **Non-Realism**. These umbrella categories indicate the degree to which the writer first, and the production team later, builds the imaginative world. Theatrical Realism, sometimes also referred to as Illusionistic or Representational, seeks to create the illusion of daily, lived experiences or at least to represent it. This is not to be confused with the reality in which we live or with what we like. Theatrical Realism utilizes recognizable, three-dimensional characters who speak in a language fairly close to the given time period and who talk about everyday concerns like jobs, money, marriage, and the like.

Clues to Realism	Clues to Non-Realism
Tightly constructed plot	Loosely constructed plot
Setting(s), costume(s), and dialogue all reveal/reflect character	Setting(s), costume(s), and dialogue that are overly theatrical
Does not break fourth wall	Breaks fourth wall through direct address or asides
Focuses on the individual and the inner psychology of said individuals	Focuses on the journy of the individual
Tries to replicate elements of everyday life onstage	Is more interested in expressing a metaphor or idea than replicating elements of everyday life
Often has characters with recognizable names (i.e., Willy, Agnes)	Often has characters named for/by their functions (i.e., Daddy, Mommy)

Fig. 1-9—Clues to Realism and Non-Realism

The settings for these pieces attempt to draw us into the lives of the characters and are detailed with objects from "real life." The characters never "break" the **fourth wall** (imagine the stage as a room from which one wall has been removed so we can view the action) to address us directly, or even to acknowledge that we are present. We become "eavesdroppers," noting character interactions within the world of the script. Non-Realism, sometimes also referred to as non-Illusionistic or Presentational, does not attempt to create the illusion of daily, lived experiences. Non-Realism acknowledges that what is being read or seen is not "real." Non-Realism also makes no effort to disguise the fact that a script is indeed a text with readers and that live theatre is indeed happening in the moment with people watching. Often Non-Realism breaks the fourth wall by having characters speak directly to the audience. These pieces are often farfetched in plot, have language that is unlike common speech and may employ character names that

Exercise #10

(Re)Presentational Theatre and "Little Red Riding Hood"

Instructions: *In groups or individually, create plans for Representational & Presentational staged versions of "Little Red Riding Hood" or another familiar story of your choice.*

- ► How would the characters have to be adapted and changed, depending on the category?
- ► What would the set look like?
- ► How would the script be adapted?
- ► Linear plot line?
- ► Episodic or mosaic structure?
- ► Addition of narrator?
- ► Addition of audience interaction/participation?

describe their plot function (i.e. Baker's Wife is indeed the wife of a baker).

Here, too, it might be helpful for you to review and apply concepts we mention to television programs and films. Again, while these media lack liveness, they offer good examples of the concepts we mention here. Often forms and styles converge and overlap. For example, Woody Allen films often have characters that "break the fourth wall" while Martin Scorsese films have characters that do not. View a television program or film and see if you can identify realistic versus non-realistic aspects of the production you are watching.

Ready, Set, Read!

To actively engage in the script, it is important to apply concepts we have covered so far. What follows asks you to recognize general aspects of a play's text—such as the title, character descriptions, and **given circumstances** (the who, what, when, where, why, and to what extent, of a script, character, etc.). Write in the margins or on a separate piece of paper as you read your play, including questions about anything that is confusing (for example, "Why did that character do that?"). Note repeated words, phrases, or images as well. These words, phrases, or images will become important not only as we continue with **script analysis** (the study of the script as literature), but later, when we begin to look at scripts from the standpoints of the director and designer, for example, moving the text from page to stage.

Exercise #11
Reading a Play

Instructions: *You may do this exercise individually or use a play assigned for class, taking notes, and coming together as a group to discuss these questions.*

1. Note both the title and the author. What information does the title convey? (As you read the play, see if the text includes a "title line"—a bit of dialogue when the title is spoken by a character.)

2. Open to the Cast of Characters or Characters Listing and read the descriptions. Also look for and read the notes in the script about any previous productions. What do these sections in the script reveal? Sometimes character descriptions disclose important given circumstances such as age, occupation, economic status, etc. about the characters.

3. Read the opening stage directions and envision what the world of the play looks like. As you continue to read, make sure to note all stage directions.

4. Begin to read. As you find yourself drawn into the play, write down any questions you have in the margins.

5. As you read, use the given clues to see if the play is Realistic or Non-Realistic.

6. How is the plot arranged? Linear? Non-linear or mosaic?

7. What are the given circumstances?

8. Think about the play's thematic concerns. Are there repeated words or images?

9. Identify the kinds of characters in the piece.

With this information fresh in your mind, turn to Exercise 12 and Exercise 13. In them, we ask you to apply terms we have already covered and introduce a few more terms and concepts that will increase your ability to talk about plays that you have read. We also have an exercise that relates to a play's action and potential metaphor(s). Remember that in Theatrical Realism the characters speak in recognizable ways (maybe from another era, but the language is close enough to our own for us to relate). The world in which the characters live is close to "real life" for their time and place—real furniture, likely walls, etc. Also, the action in a realistic play generally progresses in a linear fashion with one action or event leading to another action or event. Then, even if you are not necessarily completing these as part of a formal learning session, review what is being asked of you and reflect on the information provided here as well as that information you gather from your reading.

For both Realism and non-Realism, it is often helpful to track images in terms of both kind and number. One way to begin image tracking is to express your "gut reaction" to the overall play. Your reaction might be stated as a metaphor (comparison) or as it relates to the five

Exercise #12
Analysis of Realism

Instructions: *You may do this exercise individually or use a play assigned for class, taking notes, and coming together as a group to discuss these questions.*

1. List what the initial exposition tells you about the given circumstances of the play as you enter it. In play analysis this is often known as **stasis**, or the way things are.
2. Identify what breaks up the stasis.
3. Using the triangle of rising and falling action presented earlier (Fig. 1-5), draw the play's structure.
4. What happens at the middle of the play?
5. Figure out what major question you are waiting to have answered as you read the play (major dramatic question).
6. Note the final image of the play. Write out a literal description of the moment so that someone who has not read the play could paint your final image. Identify the point from which the lead character(s) cannot return. What did they want? Did s/he get it?

Exercise #13
Analysis of Non-Realism

You may do this exercise individually or in a group.

1. What/Where, specifically, is the beginning, middle, and end? Provide examples.
2. Is the play driven by metaphor (comparison), idea(s), image(s), plot, or other elements? List examples that support your choice(s).
3. Note how the scenes are connected. What are some emergent patterns?
4. Draw a picture of what the plot looks like based on this information.

senses. You might comment on the piece's mood. Examples might include, "The play made me think of an old lady's cloth handkerchief" or "It seemed swampy or damp" or "It was gloomy." Then search for specific words or lines that gave this initial impression. Sometimes a play will repeat specific kinds of images—blood, animals, entrapment, etc.—or, specific words. Counting these examples is a useful exercise when thinking about potential conceptual images for a production. For a general impression of most repeated words, an online program like *Wordle* produces text collages that display most repeated words in larger font.

Exercise #14
Metaphor

Created by Fulton Burns

Objective: *This writing exercise is to help reveal key elements, potential concepts, metaphors, and themes of the play being explored. It can be used for play analysis or design.*

Process: Compose a 150-word description of the dramatic action of the play. You may find it helpful or even necessary to use poetic or metaphorical images in order to make your ideas more compact. A few well-chosen descriptive words or phrases say more than a much longer retelling of everything that happens in the play. Now, condense your description, based upon the original 150 words, down to:

▶ 50 words.

▶ Then, to 25 words.

▶ Then, to 10 words.

▶ Then, to the 5 key words.

The resulting phrase (or list of 5 words) can capture or crystallize your response to the play, distilling the essential idea of the play's meaning.

Closing Thoughts

This exploration has covered a lot of foundational information. We suggest going back over any portion that confused or confounded you. We recommend this because, as you will quickly find, the work in the following explorations repeatedly returns to the ideas presented here in some way, shape, or form, building on what has been introduced.

For Further Exploration

David Ball. *Backwards and Forwards: A Technical Manual for Reading Plays* (SIU Press, 1983). Print.

Suzanne Burgoyne and Patricia Downey. *Thinking Through Script Analysis* (Newburyport, MA: Focus Publishing, 2011). Print.

Ned Chaillet, Tracy C. Davis, and Sir Tyrone Guthrie. "What Is Theatre?" *Academic Room*. 27 March 2015. Web.

Anne Fliotsos. *Interpreting the Playscript: Contemplation and Analysis* (NY: Palgrave Macmillan, 2011). Print.

Ronald A. Willis. *Fragile Magic: A Guidebook for Theatre Respondents* (Newburyport, MA: Focus Publishing, 2011). Print.

EXPLORATION TWO

Playwriting & Types of Plays

*I generally start with a line of dialogue. Someone says something
and they're talking to someone else. I don't all the time know
who's talking or who they are talking to, but you take the line of
dialogue and it starts from there.*

—August Wilson, "August Wilson on Playwriting:
An Interview," *African American Review*, 93.

IMMERSION #2
Playwriting

Instructions: *Individually, using the model below, start with a simple sentence, and
begin to write a scene.*

1. Write a sentence with a subject and a verb, somebody doing something:

    Anne teaches THEA 101.

2. Add "AND":

    Anne teaches THEA 101 AND she has to set up the projector.

3. Add "BUT":

    Anne teaches THEA 101 AND she has to set up the projector
    BUT she is technologically challenged.

4. Add "BECAUSE:

    Anne teaches THEA 101 AND she has to set up the projector
    BUT she is technologically challenged BECAUSE she is old.

5. Add a little more detail to your character. What does "Anne" look like? How does
she move? How is she dressed?

6. Add **OBJECTIVE**. What does your character want?

    Anne wants to show a *YouTube* clip for her class.

7. Add a problem, something that gets in the way of your character achieving his/her
objective, an **OBSTACLE**.

    Anne plugs in the projector and is thrown across the room—electric shock!

    Share with someone what you have written so far. (Swap)

8. Working in pairs and using your two characters, agree upon a location and create
DIALOGUE (lines for them to speak) and **ACTION** (things for them to do). Begin
writing a scene. Remember information from Chapter One as you work together
to craft your piece. You might want to be clear as to who is your lead character,
who is the antagonist, etc.

9. When your scene is completed, put it in proper play script format (see Fig. 2-3).

    You have written a short play!

Exploration Two focuses on language—ways in which playwrights and/or members of an ensemble working together to devise pieces use words to create scripts or at least outlines that will serve as the blueprint for a larger live theatrical event.

The playwright is central to the watching process in theatre because without some sort of blueprint for the world on stage there is no event for reviewers or for spectators to attend. There is a lot we can never understand about the inspiration for writing a script, so there can be no single "right way" to do it. Writers use daily experiences, observations, research, and subconscious impulses when writing scripts. Playwriting is drastically different from writing a novel or short story or even drafting a poem, in part because a script is an inspiration for something more to come—it is in the seeing of a play that the written text reaches its fullest potential. Preparing such a document takes a special person (or group) with a special drive.

A key to how special lies in the spelling of the word "playwright." *The Oxford English Dictionary* tells us that the suffix "wright" refers to an artisan or craftsperson. Just as a wheelwright is someone dedicated to the craft of making wheels and the wainwright shapes lumber to make wagons, the **playwright** is someone dedicated to crafting words and shaping incidents to make plays. As the verb "write" indicates, the process of crafting and shaping these words and incidents is known as **playwriting**. The functions of the writer in theatre are varied. In Shakespeare's time, the writer led a troupe and not only came up with characters and storylines but also coached performers. Over the course of the last three hundred years, however, the role of the single playwright has become much more isolated from the overall production process. This is probably due to printing and duplicating technologies making the dissemination of scripts much easier. Today it is possible to send electronic files across the globe in little more than a second. Some playwrights, though, still work locally, even directing the premiere production of scripts they write for a specific company of performers. No matter what process s/he follows, anyone who self-identifies as a playwright is inspired by what is around them.

So, where do playwrights come from exactly? The simplest answer is, from anywhere. Some writers are people "of the theatre" who have studied playwriting in college or have worked with theatre companies their whole lives. Others come to playwriting from different fields of interest, like the visual arts or poetry. So what does this indicate? Perhaps it tells us that all of us have the potential to be playwrights. We engage in dialogue. We have conflict. We find resolutions. We naturally want to tell our stories to others. We might even use outlets such as *Facebook* or *LinkedIn* to create a character, or at least a set of given circumstances, about who we are and how we want to be seen. What separates those who craft scripts for the stage from many of us is their ability to stay disciplined over time as a piece moves (often slowly) from an idea to a structured pattern of dialogue and physical action(s).

Thinking Theatrically

The journey from idea to page to stage can be a long one, and especially difficult if the writer is not well equipped to think theatrically. Thinking theatrically involves a consistent return to review elements of craft in order to make sure that the piece is truly written for theatre and not for film or television, each of which have their own **conventions** (a set of rules or techniques recognized, understood, and accepted by watchers). Playwriting means thinking not only about what is said but also about who says it and how. The playwriting process demands imagining a complete world with its own rules and regulations, sounds and sights, smells and tastes, and requires that an individual figure out how to have those elements happen in real time in front of spectators as performers and technicians work their magic. Playwrights have many forms from which to choose across a wide spectrum ranging from Realism to Non-Realism, tragedy to comedy. In the following section we will explore some of the challenges playwrights face as they contemplate their work.

Writing a first draft—even figuring out where to begin—may be terrifying for the nascent playwright and sometimes still daunting for those with a great deal of experience. Brainstorming ideas, though, is

Exercise #15
Brainstorming Ideas for a Play

There are many ways a playwright might generate an idea for a new play—probably as many ideas as there are playwrights. Pretend you are a playwright and try some of the following triggers for inspiration.

- ▶ Search online for an "inspirational image". This may be a photograph of people, or a painting, or a nature scene. Think of a story that the picture might tell.

- ▶ Read a newspaper or magazine. Find a story or headline that might serve as the beginning of a play.

- ▶ Recall and replay a piece of music you love.

- ▶ Think of issues that concern you. These can be personal or societal, like global warming.

- ▶ Think of a "great" line you have heard someone say.

Now, try to write a sentence that expresses what your play will be about. This sentence can be about plot, character, idea, or all three.

always a starting point for beginning to write a play. Oftentimes an idea takes many twists and turns before it emerges as a blueprint ready for public review.

Since a brainstormed idea is often shaped into a specific length, genre (type or kind), and tone as part of certain storytelling goals, it is important for us to remember that plays are categorized not only by form (realistic/non-realistic; tragedy/comedy) but also by length or duration. Playwrights craft pieces that are full-length plays, one-acts, ten-minutes, or even shorter. A scene based on the Immersion that began this chapter was in a short form. If a writer were to follow through and revise, polish, and expand that same scene, then they might be able to produce a piece of greater length and specific genre. A professional playwright might initially write a one-act play to get the idea out on paper and then later revise it into a full-length piece given the complexities at hand.

Playwriting classes offer a variety of exercises as do the many playwriting textbooks available so we will only scratch the surface here. Exercise 16 focuses on crafting the **monologue**, a speech delivered by a single character (as opposed to conversation or dialogue).

Monologues (and short plays written as monologues) serve a particular purpose with regard to the character speaking, and are about both crafting the incidents or events of a particular story to be told and the act of telling the story itself (the character narrating and his/her given circumstances). So, analyzing a monologue (or monologue

Exercise #16
Writing the Monologue

This exercise is meant for groups of six or more. If you are working alone, then generate at least three ideas/sayings to keep it interesting.

1. On one slip of paper write a common saying like, "The grass is greener on the other side."
2. On another slip of paper write a direct observation like, "The car is pea green."
3. Place the "saying slips" together and the "observation slips" together.
4. Reach into your bag or pocket, pull out an object, and place it in front of you.
5. Draw one "saying slip" and one "observation slip." The saying is your first line. The observation is your last line. The object must be revealed somewhere in the middle.
6. Set a timer for seven minutes. Begin writing. If you get stumped, then write "What I mean to say is . . ." to get back on track. Do not stop writing, whatever you do.
7. Once the timer goes off, read what you have out loud. Pay close attention to exposition and given circumstances as you read. This is the start of the revision process.

play) requires that we keep the character's backstory in mind as those events "add life" to the piece while also realizing that monologues have a purpose for the character in voicing his/her thoughts, which prompts them to openly express objectives/wants/desires to another (fictively or not) when they are speaking. Therefore, in the end, monologues express details that need to be expressed. Put another way, they reflect objectives, wants, or desires that the character has to express to a listener, for whatever reason.

Exercise #17
Analyzing the Monologue

The following worksheet returns to Aristotle's six elements as a starting point when revising a monologue you have written. It can also be useful when analyzing another author's monologue you encounter as a reader.

	Story Being Told in Monologue	Speaker (Teller of Story)
Given Circumstances		
Role of Speaker to Audience?		
PLOT (Sequence of events: Linear? Episodic? Other?)		
CHARACTER(S)		
IDEA/THEME (Message sent?)		
LANGUAGE (How does the style of speech help define the speaker?)		
MUSIC (What is the soundscape—i.e., what do we hear?)		
SPECTACLE		

A Basic Model for the Writing Process

What we suggest next is a four-step approach to thinking theatrically in the context of writing a single-author play. The steps include: getting started, revising, hearing the play aloud, and revising based on that hearing. Like any process, the amount of time spent on each step and the variety of ways in which the steps spiral back and forth, overlap, or repeat will vary depending on the writing process. Later, we will also explore alternative playwriting models in which groups of people—ensembles—work together to devise blueprints for production. We present the writing process here in a linear fashion because there is really no other way to express it on the printed page. Remember, the writing process continues in a variety of ways and often spirals around and around with several twists and turns.

Starting

We should note that the writing process itself is something to be studied in ways that we cannot here. The sheer number of playwriting books available indicates the craft inherent to the writing process. Regardless of training and study, getting started can be quite tough. The blank page stares back at you as if taunting, "I dare you to put something down." You respond, "I would like to but I have only half an idea." There are strategies, though, that can be useful in moving from a half-idea to a seed for a play and from a seed for a play to a complete text. First, consider choosing a narrow subject to explore. For example, a writer hears a story about an alcohol-fueled party culture at a local university and how social networking sites are being used to spread illicit videos of party-goers. The more the writer thinks about the story, the more s/he is intrigued by the interrelatedness of technology, popularity, and body image. Of the three, body image is the primary element of focus so the writer will do the same in the play, emphasizing the ramifications of using technology to influence public perceptions of "hot" and "not." As the idea continues to take shape, the writer establishes a one-sentence "purpose statement" that will serve as a guide. It reads, "In this play I intend to explore both a cultural dependence on technology in making 'reality' and the risk of cultural seduction that comes with this dependence." With both a focus and an emphasis clearly stated, the writer thinks about what type of plot structure might be best for the tale. At this point s/he is concerned with issues of Realism, Non-Realism, or the use of both in a hybrid play that combines aspects of each form. The writer decides that, since the idea is based on a contemporary event, the play should start out as a piece of Realism. There are six women in the original story so the first draft will start with the same, one of whom is only seen in a *YouTube*

A Basic Model for the Writing Process

Start

1. Choose a subject and then narrow your focus.
2. Develop a purpose statement as a guide for the first draft.
3. Think about both form and style as each has conventions to be followed.
4. Once started it may take weeks, months, or even years for your initial draft to be done.

Revise

1. Review setting descriptions to see if they paint a clear picture.
2. Review situations to see if they are revealing information while moving the text forward.
3. Review speaking patterns of characters as well as given attributes to see if they fit type.
4. Review other selections made in areas such as form and genre.

Hear

1. Set up some sort of public reading to get the play out of your head. (First Reading, Cold Reading, Staged Reading)
2. Actively listen to your play as it is and make notes on what is working and what is not working.

Finish

1. Stop writing and revising long enough to put the play in front of watchers for response. A workshop production in college/university environments is a good first step.
2. Collect comments from watchers, evaluate the status of the manuscript, and take time to enjoy the fact that you have a finished play, no matter what the length.

Fig. 2-1—The Writing Process

video. Finally, the writer establishes distinct points of view for the six characters. Ultimately, they will have differing ideas about the same statement: "People present themselves online in ways that are not true in person." The writer is ready and eager to begin a first draft.

Revising

There is something to be said for the adage about a writer's work never really being done. Playwrights spend years honing their craft, letting scripts they have worked on lie dormant for periods of time, returning to them, or, alternatively, revising rapidly before or right after staged readings.

With the first draft of the play now done, the writer returns to the text and begins to refine the world that has been created. One easy place to start revising is with the setting descriptions. Are they detailed

Broad Genres

Traditional Tragedy *Derived from Athenian Drama*	Modern Tragedy *Derived from "Tragedy and the Common Man"*
Hero is a person of stature	Hero is a common man or woman
No way out for hero as dictated by fate	Hero is ready to die for dignity of family or self
Hero takes responsibility for actions	Hero has the chance to come out on top right up until the end, fate has dictated nothing
Misses the mark with decisions (Hamartia)	The total evaluation of self is what makes the hero "tragic", this is how they "miss the mark"
Elevated language is used	Vernacular is used
Comedy	**Tragicomedy**
Questions what culture should be by examining humanity and society	A blending of elements found in tragedy and comedy
Begins with a flawed society that ends up balanced in some way	The extent to which these elements are mixed and how they come together is often dictated by the period in which the play is written.
Natural law and logic are often suspended	
Has a strong comic premise: accepted notions are turned upside down, usually leading to exaggeration, incongruity, and juxtaposition	
Does not have to prompt laughter per se, but does have to end with a party or some sort of pairing off	

Fig. 2-2—Genres and Their Characteristics

enough? Do they paint a full picture of place, space, and time? Are there descriptive elements that are not necessary to the narrative (to telling the story) but that do offer a deeper understanding of this world? Another important aspect to explore is situation(s). Do the happenings make sense in context? How do characters get into and out of each situation? Is it clear how each situation presented works inside the plot as part of the larger story? Part of this, then, is also consideration of tone. Is it serious? Humorous? A little bit of both of these? Figuring this out provides a sense of what type or kind of play (genre) is being written. Since each genre has its own rules, making sure the script is working inside of those parameters is an important part of revising any draft.

Exercise #18
Exploring Genre

Once again, we turn to one of the stories we used in previous exercises—"Three Little Pigs," "Cinderella," "Little Red Riding Hood," or another familiar tale of your choice. This time, we will use the story to explore genre.

1. Review Fig. 2-2. Now, create a version of the story that meets criteria for TRAGEDY. See how you can turn the protagonist into a **tragic hero** (someone of high stature, like a prince, and who makes a mistake). Make sure in this version of the story that the protagonist DOES NOT get what s/he desires, try as s/he might. You may alter the story to change which character is the protagonist, even give a twist to the plot.

2. Next, take the same story and see how you can rework it to be a COMEDY, complete with a union or even a marriage at the end. Make sure the protagonist goes through a series of trials and tribulations, but this time allow him/her to "come out on top."

3. Discuss how this exercise made the two major genres—TRAGEDY and COMEDY— understandable.

4. See what might happen if you create a mixed genre—maybe have your protagonist go through a series of complications that seem to indicate s/he will win out in the end and then end with a twist.

5. Review the earlier section on Realism versus Non-Realism and try experimenting to create, for example, a non-realistic tragedy or a realistic comedy.

Tightening the plot is an important aspect of revision. Is the plot revealing story? Is forward motion intended, or is the playwright working to establish stasis or even boredom? Is there an identifiable moment of revelation from which a character or characters can never return? Another key to unlocking revision areas is to look at characters. Are they different enough from one another to create conflict? Do they come off as truthful? Do they contribute to the story? Repeat this questioning and refining process as needed.

Although playwriting might be considered more "creative" than writing a paper, you can relate the revision process in writing a paper (when your instructor, for example, requires a rough draft and then comments on it) with that of revising a play. The playwright needs to reflect on organization (i.e. the coherence of the order of events) and must trim excess material or "tighten up" the same way we do when revising an academic paper.

The chart in Fig. 2-2 illustrates some broad genres and their characteristics. Read through the chart. If you have not yet read a variety of plays, then think about how the principles you are reading apply to films or television shows with which you are familiar. Understanding these four broad genres is crucial to both playwriting and play analysis.

```
                        ACT ONE
                       SCENE ONE

          The scene description goes here. Since the left
          margin is set at 1.5 inches, this is roughly
          indented another 1.5 inches. This is where the
          writer provides the basics for the given scene,
          including location, time of day, what technical
          elements are needed at the top of the scene, and
          the like.

                         WRITER
Notice how each character name is indented, almost to center. It
is also okay to center them. Just make sure to put the name in all
caps as a way to indicate who is speaking.

                         READER
I see that this is in Courier New font. I like to use Times New
Roman though.

                         WRITER
        (Turning to READER)
That is fine too. See how the character action tied to your dialogue
is just left of my name?

                         READER
Yes. You should look at how the staging directions are communicated
and why.

          (Staging directions are usually located in this
          position and describe entrances, exits, major
          movements or fights, technical elements that
          change . . . being chased by a giant cheese
          wedge. Just checking to see if you were reading.)

                         WRITER
Interesting.

                         READER
All of this so that I can get a sense of one minute per page while
reading. Nice.
```

Fig. 2-3—A Basic Play Page Format

For Aristotle, there were only two kinds of plays, tragedy and comedy. Today, though, there are many, many more.

A loose principle for differentiating between the two broad genres of tragedy and comedy is that most often the lead character (aka protagonist) in a tragedy fails to obtain his/her goal, whereas in comedy s/he does. We took this pause to consider genre because the playwright must be aware of how genre influences form.

Hearing

One of the best ways for a writer to get out of her/his head when writing a play is to have the text read aloud in some sort of public reading. This "hearing" part of script development can take multiple forms and happen in a variety of venues. Since plays are meant to be performed this is a natural part of the playwriting process. A **first reading** is the most informal public reading, with minimal preparation and no rehearsals, set perhaps in a classroom or in someone's living room. For a **cold reading**, performers are given scripts and sit at either music stands or at a table and read the play for an invited group of spectators "cold"—with little rehearsal. There is a clear delineation of performer and spectator, and stage directions are often read aloud. Physical movement is not a large part of this type of reading, although there may be some, along with eye contact. The primary goal of this type of reading is to clarify the overall arc of the plot, understand character relationships better, and identify irrelevant material that should be cut. A **staged reading** features performers with scripts in hand. Though lines are not necessarily memorized, the staged reading emulates a full staging by focusing on how the text might feed the efforts of a production team. Rehearsals may last for a few hours or for a week depending on the producing organization. Any of these reading styles will offer a writer deeper insight into the dialogue they have created. This is phenomenally important because it is the language of a play that creates meaning.

Finishing

No matter how much a writer works at thinking theatrically, if they never finish the play then no one will get a chance to respond to all the work they put into the process. As a writer continues to think theatrically over the course of a career, her/his ability to follow through on the overarching process described above does not necessarily get easier, but it does get refined with practice. Writing every day and revisiting elements of craft are the best ways for a writer to continually produce material that makes it to the stage.

Devised Theatre

Devised theatre is frequently done by an **ensemble** (a group of artists working together), rather than a lone writer. In this type of writing, idea (or at least theme) usually comes first, and form follows. This is because it is a topic of concern—like "American Dream"—rather than a story that is important to explore. The major question that a group must address before they create a devised piece remains the same question any producing organization must answer when choosing plays: Why this piece, for these people at this time?

Once an idea exists, it is important to remember that there is no "right" way to begin devising. One way that is commonly used, though, is brainstorming through free association of words based on a given question (i.e. what does it mean to be post-racial?). Some groups begin with improvisation or with theatre games to physicalize the brainstorming. Some begin with free writing. Some begin with other forms of combined writing and movement. One brainstorming technique we have found useful in our own devising is the use of large pieces of paper (or a white/chalkboard) to list responses, literally surrounding the ensemble with the brainstorming ideas. Often, devised theatre has at its core some pressing social issue. Many times a group devising will examine facts and figures—data—as part of their work on a piece. Sometimes they will turn to real life subjects and, as in some devised plays, to pre-existing speeches or writings. Many groups combine solo writing with interviews and gathering data with physical movements or images as they begin the creative process.

Exercise #19
Physical Theatre and Preparing to Devise

We return, yet again, to our well-known story or fairy tale. This time, though, although you will keep the story as it is, you will emphasize physical action.

1. Working in small groups, break the story down into a series of principle actions as you did before. Using the entire group, or dividing your group into pairs, assign major actions.

2. Create a tableau or frozen picture that embodies or captures the essence of each major action in the story. One person begins to read the story aloud. As s/he reaches each major action in the story, stop and have the smaller groups stage their tableau. Perhaps you can perform stories with tableaux for the rest of the class.

3. **Discuss:** How did the pictures help put the story across to the audience? How did creating or devising the pictures give you insight into the main actions of the piece? How was this experience different from the ones you had with the story earlier?

Many times devised theatre is physical in nature, with emphasis on the performers' bodies, often as they work together to create images. Perhaps many of us played "Statue Man" as children, or something like "Freeze Tag." These seemingly simple games can be a useful source of inspiration in the early stages of devising, and images created may even find their way into the final live performance. Some of you may have seen or even participated in improvisational theatre exercises. Techniques from these exercises are useful to devising as well. It is important to note that devised theatre is not the same as "improv" although it may utilize similar exercises in its inception. There are many from the realm of **creative dramatics** (imaginative and enacted works concerned with the experience of participants and not a final product) that also become useful in the creation of devised theatre, depending on the ensemble.

Before creating any devised piece, collaborators must address the skill of **transformation**, a smooth physical transition from one idea, short scene, or tableau to the next. We consider this by breaking "Freeze Tag," a well-known theatre game, into its component parts. This training game is often played in improvisational theatre classes without notice of the important skills it can build. We foreground those important skills here as they pertain to devising a theatre piece.

We pause here to suggest ways to go about creating tableaux—still images or a frozen picture—as they relate to devising a theatre piece. The still image exercise "Statue Man" can be played in a variety of ways, but the most common involves partners. One partner swings the other one around gently, releases, and the second partner (the one swung around) lands gently in a position and "freezes." The first player (and anyone else involved in the game) then identifies what the "statue" person might represent—a monkey in a cage, the Statue of Liberty, a wrestler, etc. This Frozen Picture exercise, then, can be expanded in a number of ways depending on what collaborators are interested in devising.

The end result of any or all of the writing processes we have discussed in this chapter is the same: creation of blueprint for live performance. In their final forms (as written) and in their performance (as seen) we can look at each in terms of Aristotle's six elements and determine which of them takes priority. Plot, character, idea, language, music, and spectacle are present in every theatrical production we read and/or see—traditional plays (linear or episodic), monologue performances, language-based plays, devised pieces, and more.

Exercise #20
"Freeze Tag" and Transformation

1. Two people take the stage. They choose or are assigned a situation that they will physically embody (i.e. doing the dishes together, one person teaching the other a sport—golf swing, dance step, a particular exercise). This exercise is done in complete silence, with no dialogue, so you can focus on the physical transition as you move from one picture to another and various members of the group swap places and participate.

2. The two participants take their positions. They silently execute their activity, paying particular attention to its physicality. The instructor calls "Freeze!" and the partners remain frozen in the middle of the selected activity.

3. As a group, led by the instructor, the class discusses how the physical positioning of the participants makes the activity instantly recognizable.

4. Led by the instructor, the class discusses how some aspect(s) of the tableau hint at some other activity (i.e. the way one partner reaches up might recall another sport or another familiar motion involved with, for example, placing items on a tall shelf or getting ready to swing from the branch of a tree, or reach for support on a climbing wall). Discuss these possible similarities.

5. The instructor asks for a new volunteer and the new participant taps one of the players on the shoulder, takes his/her place, and smoothly changes the activity to the new one discussed in #4. That change in position from one participant to another is a transformation.

6. Repeat, going slowly at first, allowing the second activity to resume, calling "Freeze!" and having the class discuss what the next activity might be, then tagging one of the participants, etc.

7. Gradually speed up the process, but slow down if actions become sloppy or unclear because the focus here should be on making the activity instantly recognizable.

8. At full speed, once an activity becomes obvious and a student sees the possibility for a physical transition, s/he may call "Freeze!" and tag someone out.

While this exercise is fun and often elicits laughter, it is vital that the primary objective remain making clean transitions from one tableau to the next. This is why this version of "Freeze Tag" is executed without dialogue.

Exercise #21
Devised Theatre (a longer project)

Created by Becca Worley

In groups, you will create a devised theatre piece which focuses upon an idea or theme of your choice. This can be a general theme (love, magic, nature, fear, etc.) Use the Ideas/ Inspirations guide below in your devising process. Your devised pieces must include:

- ▶ Tableau(x): Consider the whole environment of the piece: Costumes, Props, Set
- ▶ Text at the beginning and at the end of the piece: Words, Sentences: May come from music or poetry
- ▶ Transformation: a smooth move from one moment to another
- ▶ Repetition in movement and/or text
- ▶ A prop/item which is of significance to your theme
- ▶ A symbolic gesture

Consider using:

- ▶ Puppetry/Shadow Puppets
- ▶ Music, Poetry, Imagery
- ▶ Non-traditional spaces for performance

Each scene should be no longer than three minutes in length when performed, but the devising time will be much longer.

Fig. 2-4—SIU Theatre 101 Students Utilizing Physical Theatre as They Prepare to Devise

Exercise #22
Devised Theatre with a Social Conscience

In executing this exercise, your piece may focus on a political/social issue (the environment, the economy, etc.) or it can be inspired by a newspaper headline.

As a group, identify the PROBLEM you wish to address. Here is where you might turn to newspaper or magazine articles, a television or film documentary, or other sources for inspiration.

1. DISCUSS the issues you wish to address and share relevant STORIES. These may be from personal experience or from the kinds of sources mentioned above.

2. Determine a collective GOAL (i.e.: Decide the audience you need to reach and WHAT IMPACT you want to have on them).

3. BRAINSTORM ideas about how to reach that audience.
   ▶ Discuss which stories, examples, situations, characters, etc., to employ.
   ▶ Discuss the tone of your piece: funny, dramatic, light-hearted, hard-hitting, etc.
   ▶ Discuss what media to use: music, found objects, images (media or images you create), poetry, etc.

4. RESEARCH
   ▶ Draw from what's already out there, build on it. Do not reinvent the wheel.
   ▶ Learn as much as possible about your issue: from psychological, historical, sociological, political, literary, and artistic (etc.) perspectives.

5. CREATE
   ▶ Work individually and collectively.
   ▶ Try group writing exercises. Create tableaux.
   ▶ Discuss, share stories, improvise/act out scenes, fictional or based on real life.
   ▶ Work together on editing the performance text and making decisions about staging and other possible production elements, such as: music, sets, props, costumes, masks, puppets, video, etc.
   ▶ Your final live, devised performance may include a few short scenes. Remember to focus on making smooth transitions.

   The product of your work needs to be looked at from many angles: Can it be misinterpreted? Are you saying what you think you're saying? Are you respectful of your audience? Is it engaging?

6. PRESENT

Closing Thoughts

Although we have only scratched the proverbial surface here, we hope that you have a clearer impression as to why playwrights are valued members of the larger community of collaborators. In Exploration Three we will begin to examine how the literature skills we have already discussed help us to take the blueprint and move it off the page and move it on to the stage in full, live production.

For Further Exploration

Tina Bicat and Chris Baldwin, eds. *Devised and Collaborative Theatre: A Practical Guide* (Wilshire, UK: Crowood Press Ltd., 2002/2010). Print.

Gary Garrison. *A More Perfect Ten: Writing and Producing the Ten-Minute Play* (Newburyport, MA: Focus Publishing, 2008). Print.

Deirdre Heddon and Jane Milling. *Devising Performance: A Critical History* (New York: Palgrave Macmillan, 2006). Print.

Alison Oddey. *Devising Theatre: A Practical and Theoretical Handbook* (London: Routledge, 1994). Print.

EXPLORATION THREE

Designers & the Scenographic Imagination

The particular materials and resources which scenography draws upon overlap with those of theatre design. Broadly, these include scenic environments, objects, costumes, light and sound. However, because scenography focuses more on performance, other elements become equally important. Consideration of space and time are central to scenography.

—Joslin McKinney and Philip Butterworth, *The Cambridge Introduction to Scenography*, 6.

IMMERSION #3
The Scenographic Imagination, Mood & Environment

1. Recall a favorite place. This can be any place, inside or outside, but it needs to be specific.
2. Write a vivid description of that place, including both the sounds and the light. Challenge yourself to remember specific details like how the sunlight played on the leaves in a garden, or the wind rustled through the trees. Be specific.
3. Describe the colors and textures.
4. Consider what mood was created or how you felt when in that environment. How did you feel? Why?

In this exploration we take a look at the overlapping elements that comprise **scenography** —the art of creating entire performance environments primarily using structure, space, light, costume, and sound— the "total package." Another way to think about it is in terms of how a piece looks on stage in its entirety—its *mise en scène*. We focus on set, light, costume, and sound design, and how designers in each of these separate areas go about their work in order to arrive at a **unified production**, which is, again, a seamless combination of creativity that produces a live performance that looks and sounds like it belongs together. To tackle all of this, we begin with a look at an overall process of developing a scenographic imagination—a way of seeing the world of the play onstage. This chapter focuses primarily on Aristotle's elements of music and spectacle as they work together to support the play's ideas or themes. We first address the traditional design process where designers work as part of an entire production team. Generally speaking, the director leads the team as an artistic manager of sort. Moreover, the design team meets both as a group and through individual appointments with one another to make sure they are all working toward a unified production.

Exercise #23
Visual Metaphor and Inspirational Images

Often times designers are asked to respond to a play with a simple statement of how the play made them feel (i.e. "The play made me feel all hot and sweaty" or "The play was dark" or "The play made me think of a fancy Valentine"). These kinds of statements can help lead to a visual metaphor (i.e. "The road was a ribbon of light"). In this exercise you move from words and sentences to images.

These images can be abstract. Inspirational images for a play that evoke feelings of delight, for example, need not be pictures that illustrate the play's action. In fact, they should not be literal. The idea is not to search for images of the play but, rather, to search for images that speak to the play instead of the play itself. For example, for *Oedipus Rex*, a designer will not search for inspiration by googling Oedipus but might turn to words like pride or fate. For one play, you might turn to color and find images filled with yellows or pinks. For another, you might find a picture of a person with a warm and engaging smile. Use your imagination. Search engines like *Google* and *Bing* work well. Prepare an explanation of why and how these images appeal to you with regard to the play.

Note: A similar exercise can be done without a particular play by creating a set of notecards with different emotions or ideas written on them. In this version of the exercise, each student picks a random card and then goes through magazines or internet images to create a collage to describe their word.

An Overall Approach

Whether working on a scenic environment (a set), costume, lighting, or sound design, the design process is one of asking and answering questions. These questions stem not only from the script but also from the emotional and intellectual response designers have to the text. It is from this raw material that designers come up with creative solutions to many puzzles along the way, for the design elements of a production must function practically as well as artistically. While the design process is not necessarily linear, what follows is a helpful way to think about how designers move from reading a play to generating ideas to collaborating with other members of the production team in order to

An Approach to the Overall Design Process

This is freely adapted from J. Michael Gillette in Chapter Two of his *Theatrical Design and Production: An Introduction to Scenic Design and Construction, Lighting, Costume, and Makeup, 5th Edition*, 19-33.

- ▶ **Say Yes:** Making the personal commitment to serve the final production.
- ▶ **Analyze:** Gather information by reading the script at least three times.
- ▶ **Research:** Review past productions as well as historical background.
- ▶ **Percolate:** Let the information gel.
- ▶ **Choose:** Sift through all the ideas and select those most relevant to the production.
- ▶ **Execute:** Move from two dimensional paperwork to three dimensional realization.
- ▶ **Reflect:** Think about what worked, what did not, and why.

Repeat these steps as needed, always returning to the text and to information from production meetings.

Fig. 3-1—An Approach to the Overall Design Process

create a full design, realizing both their individual and the collective ideas on stage.

The most obvious place to begin is by saying "yes" to a project. In doing so you, the designer, are committing to use your skills, gifts, and talents in a way that serves the final production. Next, you begin analysis and interpretation. Gathering information from the text for further research is a large part of any analysis and interpretation process. To do this to the best of your creative ability, you will need to read the play multiple times. The first time you encounter the text read it for enjoyment, as if you were watching it. During the second reading, pay special attention to any areas of the text where you are most connected to what is happening and react to these. You might simply write them down, or you may want to find or draw an image that comes to mind or collect other images on *Pinterest* so that you can reconnect with this impulse later. These are often referred to as inspirational images. Inspirational images will help to convey ideas when meeting with the director and other members of the production team. On the third read-through of the play, consider practical design aspects and physical needs such as entrances and exits, quick changes of costumes, or rapid movement from location to location.

With both inspirational images and practical design questions in hand, complete with those questions that are unanswered, it is time to do more in-depth analysis into both the production background and the historical background of the text itself. Production background research offers insights into design pitfalls to avoid or design choices that have been particularly successful in other productions of the play. Historical research is an in-depth review of socioeconomic circumstances, geography, time, place, period, and style reflected in the script. It is also important to review form, style, genre, and theme as they relate to the written text. All of this research will eventually come to influence final creative choices made.

Percolation is perhaps one of the most important steps of design work. This may take one night, or it may take a few weeks. Nevertheless, it is important to give yourself the chance to find a clear path through the information before you choose design elements. In making these choices, you will want to sort through all of your ideas and select only those that clearly communicate your overall thinking behind the design, with specific examples of how it might look on stage (**design concept**). Of course, since all elements of production must work together, with the director guiding the process, your concept cannot clash with the rest of the production. For example, a production team might take the idea that a particular play, steeped in characters' memories, is like an old-fashioned photograph. The design concept might, then, revolve around sepia tones and blurred edges. Old photographs might serve as inspirational images for the collaborators to reference while designing so that they all work towards the same look on stage.

With your choices made, it is now time to execute the design using the appropriate paperwork, drawings, color charts, etc. Part of executing the design also includes solving practical problems that arise as the two-dimensional paperwork takes shape in the three-dimensional scenographic world. Much of this problem solving is talked about in both design meetings and production meetings where designers and other members of the production team meet, first to come up with a design and then to talk about how to make the chosen designs happen by opening night.

Elements of Successful Design

▶ The design fully serves the final production.
▶ The design is unified with the whole.
▶ The design communicates specifics about the world unfolding in live action.
▶ The design dares watchers to have more than just surface reactions.
▶ The design is dynamic, changing to match the evolving mood, tone, or content.

Fig. 3-2— Elements of Successful Design

Critics, reviewers, and watchers often come away from a live theatre event with commentary about the scenographic world they experience. But what constitutes a successful design? That type of judgment is rather subjective and can differ greatly from watcher to watcher. One of the primary indicators of a successful design, though, is how well it serves the overall production. Another good indicator of success is how detailed the final elements are and how those details communicate specifics about the world unfolding in live action. A third indicator of a design that is successful is the way it dares watchers to have more than just surface reactions to what is seen. One final element of a successful design is that of dynamism. Does the design fit an evolving mood, changing tone or the content of the piece? Does it reinforce character? Emotions? Action? While individually beautiful and revealing pieces of art, when all elements are working together does the world of the play in performance clearly communicate a unified vision?

Theatre Spaces

Starting with Ancient Egyptians and progressing until today, a variety of **theatre spaces**, formal places for live performance to occur, have emerged. Designers must be able to create for each of the major types of theatre spaces as well as for "found" spaces—spaces not created for the purpose of producing live performance but adapted for theatrical use (garages, town squares, outdoor locations, etc.). The four main types of performance spaces are Proscenium, ¾ Thrust, Arena, and Alley. There is a fifth commonly used space, Blackbox or flexible space, that can be reconfigured as one of the other types or in new and different ways.

Knowing these spaces is important to decision making when creating the design environment. The ¾ **Thrust** space is called this because it has seating on three of its four sides with the performance space jutting out into the seating area. A **Proscenium** space can also be called a picture-frame theatre because an architectural element known as an arch creates what looks like a picture frame that separates the seating area from the performance area. The **Alley theatre** space is a long walkway with seating, most often, on two sides. In *Project Runway* and *America's Next Top Model*, the "runway" is similar to an alley performance space. The way that an NBA basketball court is set up closely resembles the **Arena theatre** space, with a performance area at center and seating on all four sides. As mentioned, the **Blackbox**, or flexible space, is literally a box-shaped room painted black. This allows a producing agency to arrange the seating/performance space in any way they would like.

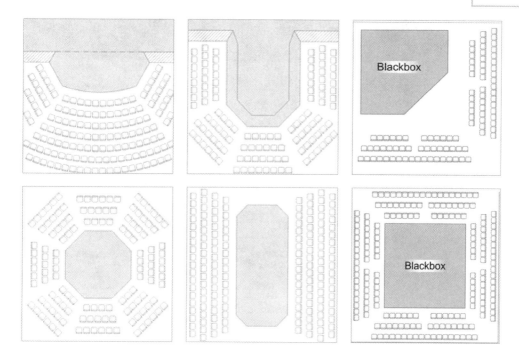

Fig. 3-3—Top Left: Proscenium, Top Center: ¾ Thrust, Top Right: Square Blackbox, Bottom Left: Arena, Bottom Center: Alley, Bottom Right: Blackbox or Flexible. *Diagrams courtesy of Anthony Reed.*

Executing the Scenic Design

The scenic environment is usually the first thing any watcher sees, and the scenic (set) designer is the person in charge of creating scenery for a performance. Before a scenic environment can be placed in a space, the designer has many choices to make, puzzles to solve, and questions to answer while working with his/her director. In executing the design it is important to determine when (period) and where (location) the scripted plot takes place not only according to the given circumstances as established in the script but also with regard to the particular production approach because the director and production team might decide to move the action from what is stated in the script to another time and place (i.e. Shakespeare's *Romeo and Juliet* in a hip suburb of Verona). It is also vital to note what the world looks like (style) and into what genre the written text might fit. Combining the given circumstances the playwright provides with emotional and artistic response(s) from reading and rereading the text allows the designer to develop a central image or scenic metaphor as part of a larger concept. Reactions from the other members of the production team will also have influence. Having made choices and discussed them with the director, the scene designer begins to generate drawings and models so that other collaborators can sense what the set will look like in the

Fig. 3-4—White Model. *Created by Dr. Ronald Naversen.*

performance space. These are shared in production meetings. As the scenic environment is being built, a designer must still be prepared to solve problems and puzzles as they arise. Solutions to these problems and puzzles come not only from the written text and research but also from the knowledge the designer has about how building materials work to create structures and space.

Executing the Scenic Design

1. Determine given circumstances.
2. Use both given circumstances and research to devise concept, central image, and/or a scenic metaphor.
3. Draft a ground plan.
4. Attend production meetings not only to solve problems but also to coordinate with the other design areas.
5. Solve puzzles and problems as they arise while the design is being built.
6. Keep reading and rereading the written text as necessary to find clues and inspiration.

Fig. 3-5—Executing the Scenic Design

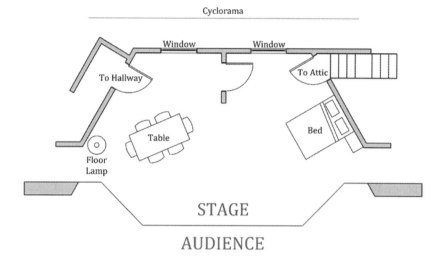

Fig. 3-6—Ground Plan. *Created by Anthony Reed.*

Methods and Materials of Scenic Design

The **ground plan** is a "bird's eye view" of the space, scenic elements, and architecture and includes the outline of walls, placement of furniture, location of door and windows, and suggested entrance and exit points—all viewed from above the theatre space. This is the primary piece of paperwork used by a scenic designer in communicating how a setting fits into a given performance space.

Another important drawing is a **front elevation**, which is the scenic environment drawn "full face." This drawing is fundamental in helping carpenters see how to build the design. A **paint elevation** is a color version of the front elevation. This drawing helps others envision a full color version of the setting. Scenic designers might also build a **white model**, which is an unpainted, scale model of the scenic environment (Fig. 3-4). All of these communication tools working together provide a clearer picture of the physical layout of the performance space.

When making sketches, drawings, and models, a designer must consider how many settings there are, how the scenery will be moved (if at all), and how much money it will cost to build the setting as drawn.

The two fundamental components of any setting are the **platform** and the **flat**. A platform is used to make floors and can be made to different heights. Traditionally made with a 2x4 lumber frame and plywood top, tubular steel and plexiglass are other options. If a platform has casters on it, then it is known as a **wagon**. A flat is used to make walls. Usually put together using a 1x4 lumber frame, there are two types of coverings for flats. A **hard covered flat** is a piece of scenery

Exercise #24
Scenic Design: The Ground Plan and Elevation

1. Using graph paper or a straight edge draw a top view of your room. Lines will represent the walls. Make sure to leave blank spaces for where doors and windows are located. Since this is a top view, a simple rectangle can stand for a bed and small squares may serve as chairs. Do not worry about exact scale; just try to keep furnishings relative to each other in size, and keep everything in a top view only. You have drawn a ground plan of your room.

2. Turn the paper and view your drawing from all four sides. Put it at eye level, and imagine what someone viewing it from a particular direction would see. A straight-on view is an elevation.

3. Now imagine how you might transform that four-sided space into a set in a Proscenium theatre space. Make choices about what has to move or be removed so the watchers can see into the world of the play.

4. Lastly, create a front view of the center area of your drawing. Try to keep furniture in relative scale (proportion) and to avoid furniture floating in space.

covered with thin plywood called lauan or Philippine mahogany. The advantage of this flat is that it not only bounces sound back towards the seating area but also lasts a long time. A **soft covered flat** is one that has a fire-treated fabric known as muslin on it. Stretched like a painter's canvas, this type of flat is lightweight and is easy to move. This flat, though, does have the tendency not only to suck up sound but also to break more easily than the hard covered flat. Flats can also be used as masking, preventing audience members from seeing into backstage areas. Painted drops, legs, and borders are also used to complete the design. These are known as "soft goods" because they are fabric based. A **drop** is a large painted background literally hung from a steel pipe (known as a **batten**) that is attached to or suspended from the grid and then dropped to the floor. **Legs** are tall, relatively skinny curtains (usually black), and **borders** are long, wide curtains (usually black) that work together both to frame the scenic environment and to hide areas watchers should not see, similar to the way a valance and curtains might in work your home windows. With technological advances, projected scenic environments are becoming more and more popular. In most cases, scenic designers can integrate film sequences and moving images into the overall environment by using technology such as *Isadora*, *Hippotizer*, *Pandora's Box*, or *Arkaos*.

Building Blocks of Scenic Design

Much of the drawing and modeling mentioned above can be done either by hand or with computer-aided design (CAD) equipment. In

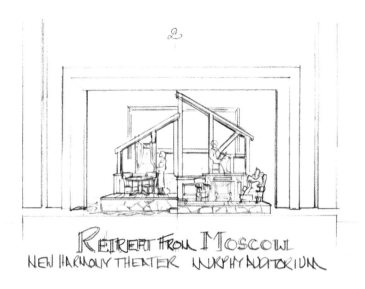

Fig. 3-7—
Full Stage Sketch.
*Created by
Dr. Ronald
Naversen.*

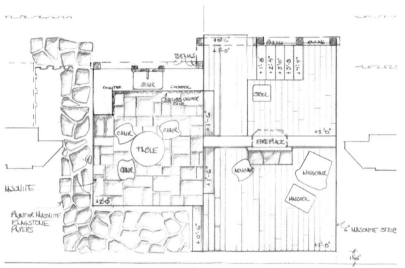

Fig. 3-8—
Ground Plan.
*Created by
Dr. Ronald
Naversen.*

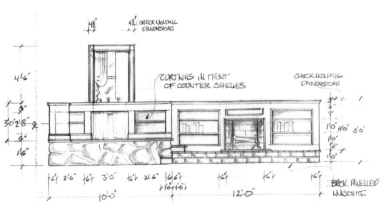

Fig. 3-9—
Front Elevation.
*Created by
Dr. Ronald
Naversen.*

either case the building blocks of scenic design remain line, mass, composition, texture, color, and value. Skilled manipulation of these building blocks is fundamental to creating a functional, interesting scenic environment.

Line is the starting point of any design as it creates a silhouette in the performance space. Whether round, angular, or somewhere in between, line can both convey meaning and guide watchers' eyes through the space. To do so, scenic designers most often use line to create geometric shapes such as triangles, hexagons, squares, rectangles, or circles. If the mood, tone, or content calls for it, then the designer can use irregular or flowing forms of natural shapes, like those of large trees. It is also possible for a scenic designer to incorporate abstract uses of line, which look like distortions.

Mass in design considers how bulky, or heavy, a setting is. Mass indicates weight. Is the set piece solid? **Composition** is putting together the pieces while considering vertical and horizontal planes and whether or not the setting needs to be balanced or asymmetrical. **Texture** is always a part of a scenic environment. It refers not only to the visual surface but also to the tactile surface of materials in use—slick, rough, fuzzy, firm.

Color is just that, and, along with **value** (density or vibrancy of the color), provides essential touches to any design. This is because the

---

The Scene Designer: Review

The Scene Designer's role clearly illustrates the ways in which each member of the production team executes tasks that are both functional and aesthetically pleasing or artistic, trying to create a unified production.

Some Building Blocks of Scenic Design Include:

- ▶ Line
- ▶ Mass
- ▶ Height
- ▶ Color
- ▶ Symmetry or Asymmetry

A major factor in the creation of a set design is the number of scene changes (different locations and the number of times they appear) the play requires and how they can be made smoothly and efficiently, while making an artistic contribution to the production as a whole.

Many designers employ what they call a "scenic metaphor" to complement the play's thematic concerns.

Fig. 3-10—The Scene Design: Review

array of colors chosen (and the value of them) work together to communicate mood while also, at times, creating drastic statements.

The Support Staff

Usually the scenic designer has help in moving from ideas and illustrations to an actual, physical environment. Three key members of the support staff include the technical director, scene shop foreman, and carpenter(s). The **technical director** is someone who not only oversees the building of the scenic design but also manages all other aspects of technical production. Some duties include budgeting for each production, keeping materials in stock, training workers in safety and procedures, keeping projects on deadline, and the like. The **scene shop foreman** is usually the person who takes charge of the scene shop area where the entire scenic environment is built. The foreman relies on **carpenter(s)** to get the set built and placed properly in the performance space. Closely related to the work of these staff members is that of the properties or prop designer. In either case, **props** (objects held or used in the production) are used to enhance the *mise-en-scène* and are sometimes vital to the play's action. The person in charge of creating them is sometimes referred to as the **props designer**.

Costume Design

Watchers arrive at live theatre expecting to see garments that tell a story and define character. A great place to begin thinking about how costumes work in live theatre is with your own clothing. Consider for a moment what your current garments say about you. What story do they tell? How do they communicate your social position or status? To what extent do they or do they not indicate gender? Occupation? When do your garments show modesty or lavishness? Do they showcase an unyielding personality or one that is free-spirited? To what extent do they indicate the occasion for which you are dressed? These types of considerations are similar to those of a costume designer as they go about creating clothing for characters in a live performance.

Executing the Costume Design

In thinking about how clothing works in live performance, the costume designer, like the scenic designer, considers several elements. One of the designer's first tasks is to identify the given circumstances not only of the text but also of each character in the plot. Just as with scenic design, this information is important when matching garments to period, place, style, and tone. The design must indicate the world we are watching even before any character speaks a line. Closely related to this, the design should indicate characterization, not just a character. Is someone in the play an ordinary or extraordinary person? Are they shy or outgoing?

Evidenced-based (from the script) decisions will influence color and fabric choices. We have included a chart that can be utilized in tracking the sorts of selections a costume designer must make based on both artistic and practical considerations.

As with scenic design, combining text-based information with emotional and artistic response(s) from reading and rereading the text allows the costume designer to develop his/her concept. This concept helps guide all choices, including how to indicate relationships among characters. Having made these selections in private, the designer needs to consult not only with the director but also with the other designers to make sure the garments are consistent with the entire world of the

Exercise #25
Deconstructing Costume Design

Contributed by Stephi Molitor Jorandby

What does your outfit communicate to others?

In this exercise, you will start with an outfit and work backwards to "decode" what cloth-ing says about the person who is wearing it.

Instructions:

1. Come to class (or try this with someone outside of class) in an outfit that really says something about YOU. It might be your letter jacket, your lucky "job interview" clothes, your hunting gear—clothes that communicate who you are as a person.

2. Partner with someone you do not know well. Introduce yourselves, but do not discuss any other information besides your names. Observe your partner's outfit. What conclusions can you draw about this person based on what s/he is wearing? Can you guess their major? Their hobbies? What about their age, religion, geographic location, job (Given Circumstances)? Write down what you learn from your partner's clothing. Be honest, kind, and fair; you are not passing judgment but, rather, simply observing.

3. Note your partner's choices in color, fabric, accessories—all the elements of Costume Design. What is unique about their outfit?

4. After both of you have had a chance to record your observations, discuss your findings. How accurate was your "decoding" of your partner's clothing in relation to who they are?

5. Share your results in small groups or with the class.

Costume Plot							
Character	Costume Changes	Fabric	Color(s)	Pattern or Print	Trim	Accessories	Notes
Name							
	1.						
	2.						
	3.						
Name							
	1.						
	2.						
Name							
	1.						
	2.						
	3.						

Fig. 3-11—Sample Costume Plot

play. Much of this happens in production meetings, either face-to-face or electronically. With all of this input it is time to turn general ideas, doodles, and sketches (often called **thumbnails**) into fully realized color drawings of character clothing (**renderings**), complete with fabric swatches. This paper trail, electronic or otherwise, aids in building the three-dimensional costume. A garment cannot be completed, however, without taking into account the performer's body and his or her movement needs. For example, designing a costume for a wheelchair bound character is different from designing a costume for an able-bodied dancer.

Methods and Materials of Costume Design

Costume renderings are a fundamental communication tool used by the costume designer. These drawings usually provide ideas for line, color, fabric choices, embellishments, and perhaps even character-specific accessories. A good deal of this kind of drawing can be done either by hand or with the help of computer software such as *Corel Painter*, *Paint Shop Pro*, *Adobe* software, or *iPad* applications. Another important drawing is the **pattern**. Either purchased in a store and adapted or drafted by the designer, a pattern provides the outline of every piece

Fig. 3-12—Color Costume Rendering with Swatches. *Courtesy of Wendi Zea.*

of a garment so that it can be built from scratch. When building a garment from scratch, a prototype is often made from muslin or canvas. This helps the designer see what adjustments need to be made to the pattern before cutting into the more expensive fabric to be used in the final costume piece. Fabric and a variety of other clothing-grade soft goods are the primary materials in costume design and construction. A good costume designer is aware of a broad range of textiles. Some types of materials frequently used include leather, cotton, wool, silk, denim, nylon, polyester, linen, jute, and rayon, to name a few options. These can be embellished with lace, ruffles, fringe, metallic ornaments, fur, feathers, and the like. Swatches of these often accompany renderings so that everyone involved in the production process can get a sense of what the final costume should look like. If not building a costume, then the designer might offer a photographic image of a garment that will be pulled from the company's stock of already-made costumes or purchased and adjusted to fit not only character but also performer. Key to all of this is the ability to bring together the building blocks of costume design through sewing, stitching, and otherwise securing pieces in ways that will hold up to the rigors of repeated live performance.

Executing the Costume Design

1. Determine period, place, style, and tone based on the written text.
2. Use both given circumstances and research to devise a concept.
3. Draft basic sketches and renderings that indicate characterization and relationships.
4. Attend production meetings not only to solve problems but also to coordinate with the other design areas.
5. Solve puzzles and problems as they arise while the design is being built, making sure each garment meets the movement needs of a given performer.
6. Keep reading and rereading the written text as necessary to find clues and inspiration.

Fig. 3-13—Executing the Costume Design

Building Blocks of Costume Design

Line, fabric, color and value, embellishments, and accessories are the building blocks of costume design. **Line** refers not only to the cut of a garment but also to the pattern or grain of a given fabric. Long ago designers figured out that using a horizontal line adds width to a character while a vertical line can either add a sense of height or indicate dignity. The diagonal line often indicates a sense of excitement or excitability. Closely related to this is **fabric** (woven or knitted fibers). Depending on the textile chosen, fabric can influence silhouette or outline, provide a sense of bulk, offer a distinct texture, or even encompass line in a pattern or grain. **Color** and **value** are also important considerations because of the psychological effect they can have on watchers. The pattern on fabric is important, too, and often beginning costume designers fail to recognize that tiny, busy patterns cannot be seen by audience members gathered in a large seating area or house. **Embellishments** or trims can be anything from fringe, lace, and ruffles to fancy buttons, zippers, and snaps. Sometimes flashier elements such as sequins, fur, or feathers are used as well. **Accessories** are items such as hats, purses, and walking sticks. These are the fine details that further delineate one character from another. Other ways that these building blocks can manifest in a design include the areas of hair, makeup, and masks. While large producing organizations may have separate individuals in charge of designing these items, more often than not they fall under the purview of the costume designer. This makes sense, though, given how each relates to character and characterization.

Exercise #26
Character, Texture, Color

Created by Casey Watkins

Costume Design & Character

Choose a character and write five words/phrases describing the character (Old maid, snob, etc.). Using copied bodies without clothes (**croquis**) and including different body types if possible, collage or draw. Use markers, colored pencils, or paints and/or pens to draw costumes on the figures based on one or more character(s) from a play you have read. Discuss how line/texture/color, etc. can inform the audience about the character(s).

You can also use collage for this exercise.

Texture & Color

Use fabric swatches of various types—everything from upholstery to chiffon—and in groups come up with a character description of the type of person who would wear something made out of each type of fabric. Be able to state why the character would wear that fabric. Continue and do the same exercise with color swatches. Now, combine texture (type of fabric), color, and trims.

We should note here that, in practice, play analysis for the costume designer operates on a practical as well as artistic level. Once the costume designer is familiar with themes and images, character, etc., s/he must plot costume changes and analyze the design from scene-to-scene to make sure that the clothing matches the action of the play.

The Costume Support Staff

The **costume shop manager** makes sure that the building of costumes stays on track and on (preferably under) budget. Like the scene shop foreman, the shop manager trains workers and relies on cutters, stitchers, and drapers to help move a design from renderings to prototype to finished garment.

These individuals are responsible for cutting out fabric/patterns, sewing, and seeing how the sewn item can best fit on a performer.

Lighting Design

The primary puzzle the lighting designer must solve is that of visibility. That is, since the primary function of light in the natural world is to illuminate objects so that living beings can distinguish one from another, the lighting designer must be able to replicate this full range

The Costume Designer: Review

Like the other designers, the costume designer works in conjunction with the rest of the production team. The costume designer must be cognizant of how the costumes will work on stage. The costume designer must pay attention to the practical considerations of the play (How many costume changes are there? Can the actors make them in time? Do the actors have to execute any gymnastic activities? Do they need to fight or dance?) as well as the aesthetic considerations of vision (idea/theme) and concept. Costumes, of course, might suit the characters' ages, genders, socioeconomic status, occupation, etc. They also might indicate the era (century, decade, year), season, or time of day reflected in the world of the play. But, the director and production team might choose to set the play in a completely different style (time, place, etc.) from the way in which it is written. Regardless, costumes (and all the design elements) must meet certain criteria.

Costumes Need To:

▶ Reveal characters' personalities and given circumstances, the reality of the world of the play, such as age, gender, health, social status, educational level, etc.

▶ Reflect mood, theme, style of production

▶ Be unified with the whole production

▶ Have psychological effect on the audience

▶ Meet the physical needs of the production's staging

Some Costume Vocabulary:

▶ **Silhouette:** The outline or general shape of garments on the body

▶ **Vertical line:** Gives a sense of height, dignity, strength

▶ **Horizontal line:** Provides a sense of width

▶ **Diagonal line:** Often indicates excitement or at least excitability

▶ **Weight:** How heavy is the fabric, particularly when placed on the body?

▶ **Texture:** What does the fabric feel like or what feeling might it evoke?

▶ **Color:** Brightness, saturation, or hue of fabric(s)

Fig. 3-14—The Costume Designer: Review

of seeing indoors. It does a watcher no good to attend any live event if the performance cannot be seen. Like the other designers, the lighting designer always begins with the reading and rereading of the written text for given circumstances information. Similar to the scenic and costume designer, the lighting designer is looking to establish time (i.e. day or night) and place (i.e. inside or outside) as well as matching the tone of the written text and the mood of each scene. As with scenic and costume design, this information, along with any artistic and emotional response(s) to the written text, allows the designer to develop a concept. With this information in hand, it is time to have a discussion

Executing the Lighting Design

1. Determine how to provide visibility using given circumstances.
2. Use both given circumstances and research to devise concept.
3. Draft appropriate drawings, computer models, and paperwork.
4. Attend production meetings not only to solve problems but also to coordinate with the other design areas.
5. Adjust initial ideas to match not only performer movements but also other design elements.
6. Watch rehearsals when necessary to solve problems and find inspiration.

Fig. 3-15—Executing the Lighting Design

about the style of production so that lighting choices can reinforce not only the directorial concept but also the other design elements. Once the lighting designer has the okay from his or her director to move forward, s/he creates drawings, chooses colors, and thinks about the placement of **light cues**, or what might simply be called changes in light.

This preliminary work can only be finalized after the lighting instruments are hung, the dimmers are **patched** (meaning electricity runs to the appropriate lighting instruments), performers arrive, and the other design elements are completed during the rehearsal process. Most of the finalizing of lighting choices is done during technical rehearsals, which are for the purpose of coordinating and refining design elements as they are integrated with performers. Because light needs something to hit in order to be appreciated, it is only after the other above mentioned elements are in place that the lighting designer can completely reinforce the overall style of production. While reading the written text can be a way to gain information in the early days of planning, it is the scenic environment, costume design, and performers' bodies moving about the space that allow for full inspiration.

Methods and Materials of Lighting Design

The light plot and cue sheet are two of the most important pieces of paperwork a lighting designer can use to communicate ideas, because they offer the best way to visualize light without ever turning on a lighting instrument. Since the **light plot** is an overhead view of the position for each lighting instrument, it can help the designer ensure that there are enough pools of light to illuminate the performance space. The **cue sheet**, paperwork on which all the lighting changes or cues are listed and described, assists the director in visualizing when light changes at any given moment in live performance. This paperwork is not only important in production meetings but also in **paper tech** (a rehearsal held off stage without actors, literally done on paper) and **cue-to-cue** (a rehearsal of changes in lighting with actors or stand-ins from beginning to end of the piece being performed). Without lighting instruments, though, most designs cannot be realized in live performance.

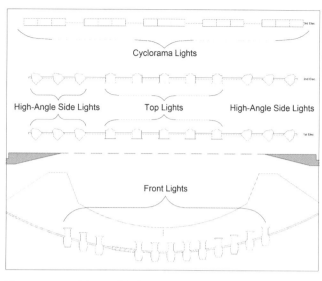

Fig. 3-16—Positions of Lights around Stage. *Courtesy of Anthony Reed.*

The two most common lighting instruments in use today are the soft-edged spotlight and the sharp-edged spotlight. Also known as a **Fresnel**, the soft-edged spotlight produces a wide beam of light and is usually used for a medium throw distance. Using a colored filter known as a **gel** can change the color of light coming from the instrument.

The **ellipsoidal reflector spotlight (ERS)** produces a sharp, concentrated beam of light. It is usually used because it has a longer throw distance and produces a sharper, more focused beam of light. The four shutters on the side of the barrel and a set of brackets on the end of the lens tube are good clues to identifying an ERS. The shutters allow manipulation of the shape of a beam of light into a square, triangle, or half-moon. The brackets at the end of the lens tube allow for the addition of accessories such as a color-changing unit. Near the top shutter there is also a slot where a steel cutout called a **gobo** can be inserted

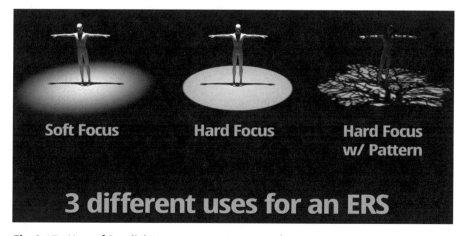

Fig. 3-17—Uses of Spotlight Instruments. *Courtesy of James Diemer.*

Light Cues			
Production Name: _____			
Designer's Name: _____			

Cue Sheet			
Date: _____			
Page _____ of _____			

Page #	Cue #	Description of Cue	Notes
5	1	Pre-show and house full	
5	2	Pre-show and house half	
5	3	Blackout	
5	4	Lights up on stage, should be amber front with hints of blue side, needs to reproduce the look of early evening	
12	5	Lights dim little, it is now deep evening, cool blue	

Fig. 3-18—Sample Cue Sheet

to mold a beam of light into the skyline of New York, a grouping of tree limbs, July 4th fireworks, or any other shape that can be cut out. It is the flexibility of the ERS that makes it one of the favorite instruments of lighting designers.

Par cans are basically "coffee cans" with lamps in them and **scoops** are large, usually round-shaped instruments that can be used to fill in areas that need more light. **Strip lights** and **border lights** are a bank of floodlights meant to illuminate broad areas like a drop. The **follow spot** is just that, a beam of light on a swivel used to follow a performer as s/he moves. More recently, designers have started using automated or **intelligent lights**. These somewhat ball-shaped instruments are computer programmed, rotate, and can do all of the operations described above, and much more. In fact, much of this advanced technology can now be controlled by *iPod* or *iPad* remotes held by the lighting designer (or an assistant) while working from one cue to another during technical rehearsals.

More and more theatre companies, colleges, and universities are adding LED (light-emitting diode) lamps to their lighting instrument inventories. LEDs are expensive to purchase, but over time, they are both more efficient and last longer than other lamps, lending appeal to the ecologically-minded in the industry. They need no warm-up time, but because they are affected by temperature, they do require cooling fans or other means of heat dissemination. Colors produced with LEDs are strongly saturated and offer lighting designer great opportunities.

The world of stage lighting will change exponentially as LED lighting not only augments but also ultimately replaces other kinds of lighting equipment we have discussed here.

The angles and placements of lighting instruments are crucial to accomplishing the sculpting effects the lighting designer desires. Both the lighting angles and positions list and images provide some of the most important positions used in live performance.

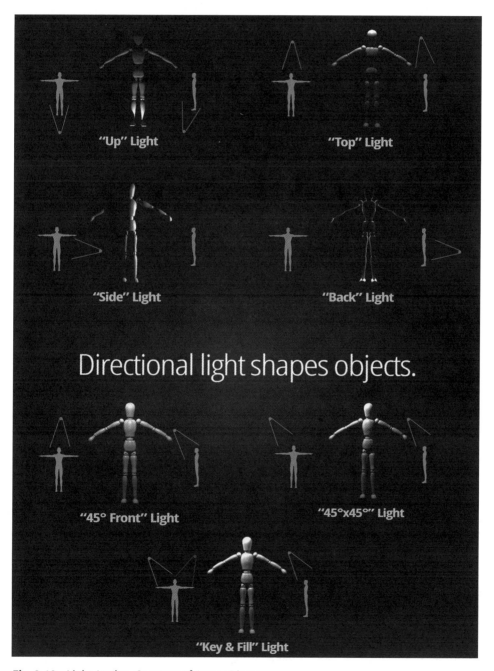

Fig. 3-19—Light Angles. *Courtesy of James Diemer.*

Building Blocks of Lighting Design

Much of the paperwork and idea generating can be done either by hand or with the aid of computer software such as *Lightwright* or *AutoPlotVW*. Whichever way the designer chooses to generate his or her paperwork, visibility, composition, mood, and reinforcement are four basic building blocks of lighting design. Lighting designers often break these down further into specific elements so that they can have more flexibility when putting finishing touches on a design. These elements include intensity, direction, color, shape, dimension, movement, and texture. The primary way to control visibility is through intensity, or degree of brightness. **Composition** in lighting design refers not only to indicating where the center of action in each scene should be but also to defining objects, persons, and their relationships. **Direction** indicates where the light is pointed or focused and what it is illuminating, while shape specifies the way a beam of light leaves the lighting instrument (i.e. round or triangular). The size of the beam as it leaves the lighting instrument is its **dimension**, and the **texture** of a light is the way it looks on a surface (i.e. "trees gobo"). **Mood** is the overall psychological effect of the scene as indicated by lighting. The easiest way to manipulate this building block is through the use of color. The lighting designer often thinks in terms of warm colors (in the red/yellow family) and cool colors (blue/green). **Reinforcement** is considering how light, working with the other design elements as well as performers, can support moment-to-moment occurrences in live performance. **Movement** is a unique way to enhance any composition by controlling how and where light appears. The more practice someone has experimenting with and manipulating of these building blocks, the easier it will be to complete a successful design.

Exercise #27
On Lighting Design

1. Bring in three art images/photos from magazines, websites, or other publications.
2. Student designers swap images so they do not have their own. Choose one.
3. Write three words that describe the emotion evoked in the images.
4. Using no more than five flashlights (or cell phones with flashlight applications) and gel scraps, recreate the emotion in color.
5. Discuss.

Now, using light, try to create a "scene." Students can make up the situation, but they must be able to describe color(s) and use at least two lighting directions. Most importantly, they need to justify their choices.

The Lighting Designer: Review

Just like the other designers, the lighting designer works in conjunction with the rest of the production team to put across an agreed-upon concept to the audience. As with the other designers, the lighting designer utilizes properties or tools specific to this production area. The lighting designer manipulates the elements or qualities of light to obtain desired effects.

The Objectives of Lighting Design:

- ▶ Provide visibility—nothing much matters if the audience cannot see!
- ▶ Help establish time and place
- ▶ Help create mood
- ▶ Reinforce the concept
- ▶ Provide focus and create visual composition—where should the audience look?
- ▶ Establish rhythm and movement

One lighting designer explains, "It is as important to make sure the audience is not looking where they should not be as it is to make them look where they should!"

The Lighting Designer must also remain cognizant of practical lighting (lamps, fireplaces, overhead lights) that must appear to be operated by switches, lights in refrigerators, and ovens, etc.

The Lighting Designer uses these Qualities of Light:

- ▶ **Intensity:** How bright or how light; establishing the intensity is called "setting levels."
- ▶ **Color:** White light is not really white. Colors must be mixed, unless, of course the designer wants the actors' skin to be colored or the fabric of the costumes to be falsely colored. The colored "plastic" that goes in front of the lamp is called a "gel."
- ▶ **Direction:** A general wash is usually established to light the stage, overall.
- ▶ **Form:** How an object is lit can help define or obscure its shape. The Lighting Designer works with the Set Designer as the Set Designer determines line, mass, etc.
- ▶ **Movement:** In essence, the Lighting Designer utilizes the elements or qualities of light to accomplish the objectives of lighting. In reading the script, the Lighting Designer notes given circumstances such as times of day, weather, location changes, etc.

Fig. 3-20—The Lighting Designer: Review

The Lighting Support Staff

The lighting designer often relies on a **master electrician** (crew head in charge of hanging the light plot) and a crew of electricians to hang, focus, and gel his or her light plot. During live performance, the **light board operator** is charged with following the cues written by the designer and called by the Stage Manager. If there is a follow spot, then there is a dedicated operator for that instrument as well. The lighting designer is often also in charge of any projections or special effects that might be called for in the production design. If this is the case, then s/he often works closely with the scenic designer to make sure all projections and effects complement the setting. Usually these design elements also have board operators or machine operators during live performance. Depending on the size and budget of a production, a **projection designer** may be brought on board to facilitate both the creation and the execution of a video design. More and more in contemporary theatre, a media/video designer is emerging as the stand-alone individual in charge of such technologies.

Thinking back to Aristotle's Elements of Drama for a moment, the set designer and costume designer address spectacle more than the other elements in search of a way to portray plot, character, and idea. The lighting designer's work is not only dealing with spectacle in that it is seen but also with music in that s/he contributes significantly to the rhythm and tempo of a production in how light moves around the performance space. It is the sound designer's job to focus almost exclusively on the element of heard music.

Sound Design

Tasks associated with sound design range from something as simple as making a rotary dial phone ring or as complex as providing vocal reinforcement for musical singers, a full orchestra, and non-singing performers to even creating underscoring or a soundscape for an entire production, like in films. The sound designer must pay attention not only to **practical sounds** called for by the production, like phones or doorbells, but also to the **implied sounds** that emerge from the **subtext** (what is meant but not said). The sound designer also thinks about offering pre-show, post-show, and intermission music. In these ways and more s/he contributes greatly to the mood of the production.

Executing the Sound Design

The biggest challenge for any sound design professional is selecting aural components that are appropriate not only to the written text but also to the overall production design. In practice this means that the sound designer is concerned with audibility of sound(s), motivation for sound(s), transition and other incidental music or sound(s), and live vocal enhancement (if needed). Like the other designers, the sound designer sets about reading and rereading of the written text for given circumstances information. Of course time of day, period, place, season, etc. are important given circumstances that must be noted when reading. This raw material is more than enough information to start a discussion with the director about the style of production, making sure that any choices reinforce not only the directorial conceit but also the other design elements. While thinking about cue placement, speaker placement, and other aspects of sound reinforcement often starts prior to rehearsals, it is not until the sound designer attends rehearsals in the performance space that he or she can fully plan how a soundscape will augment the action unfolding in live performance. As with lighting design, reading the written text can only provide so much information and inspiration. It is the collaboration of all the other elements that offers the best clues to finishing touches.

Methods and Materials of the Sound Design

The **sound cue sheet** is the primary piece of paperwork generated by the sound designer. Similar to the light cue sheet, the sound cue sheet keeps track of when an aural effect turns on, when it turns off, and what it does. Much of the sound designer's methods and materials are tied to the types of technology they have to use for a given design. Digital technologies from the 1990s, featuring mini-disks and players, DAT recorders, CDs, samplers, and eventually desktop computer software contributed greatly to the expansion of sound design. Currently software such as *iTunes* and *GarageBand*, *Metasynth*, and *Audacity* combine the recordability of the above formats with the processability of the computer. Even amplification technology inside of microphones and speakers has advanced, expanding the types of design choices

---

Executing the Sound Design

1. Determine given circumstances of the aural world.
2. Use both given circumstances and research to devise a soundscape.
3. Create appropriate tracks for text-based sounds.
4. Attend production meetings not only to solve problems but also to coordinate with the other design areas.
5. Watch rehearsals to enhance initial ideas and adjust the existing sound environment.

Fig. 3-21—Executing the Sound Design

that can be made for a live performance. These advances have afforded sound designers the same creative controllability that lighting, projection, and special effects design has had for years. Two other types of important materials include music and sound effects. Designers think about myriad ways to use music for cues or transitions and as ambient filler. Sound effects either reinforce stage action or provide information to the watcher. Three common types of effects are textual referent, atmosphere creation, and evocative response. A **textual referent** is a sound design choice taken directly from the written text while **atmosphere creation referent** refers to the use of sound or music to reinforce mood. In the context of sound design, the **evocative response** effect is a sound design choice meant to evoke emotions in a watcher as s/he sees the scene unfold. Sound designers have vast knowledge of databases, listings, and other library sources from which to pull. Though methods and materials will continue to shift at a rapid rate as technology improves, the root of inspiration remains the blueprint provided by the playwright.

Building Blocks of the Sound Design

Four building blocks of sound design include consideration of environment, audibility, duration, and route. There are two different types of sound environments—the **physical environment** and the **virtual environment**. The physical sound environment is that which we hear and deals with the physics of sound and acoustics while the virtual sound environment refers to the use of digital equipment in creating the design. **Audibility** is how loud or soft, how processed or natural the presented soundscape is in live performance. Both the duration of a certain sound effect or music cue and the route it takes to reach watchers are important considerations as well. The cruel paradox of these building blocks is that if they work well then no one notices. When they do not work, watchers are guaranteed to comment.

The Sound Support Staff

Sound design is often a solitary position. At some larger venues sound professionals are charged with hanging speakers, running cable, and wiring microphones, but in more cases than not it is the designer who handles creating the physical sound environment. As this role continues to grow and expand, there is little doubt that the support staff will as well.

Exercise #28
On Sound Design

1. Find an open scene or monologue (perhaps the one you wrote).
2. Using phone ring tones, substitute the words used in the scene with the tones that match what is meant by each line but not said (subtext).
3. Be able to explain why each tone is an appropriate replacement for the word.
4. Present your ideas.

   Make sure to think about context as you go about making your choices.

Exercise #29
On Listening

1. Listen to instrumental music of different kinds and/or recordings of sounds in nature, like those often used in meditation.
2. List the emotions these selections evoke in you and be able to explain why you feel them.
3. Develop a collage of color, images, etc. that illustrates the emotions evoked in #2.

Exercise #30
On Soundscapes

Contributed by Bevin Myake

What is a soundscape?

We often tend to isolate sounds, considering them one by one and/or separating them into categories of practical versus natural—a doorbell or telephone, a bird chirping, etc. Sound is really much more layered and nuanced. In other words, we hear more than one sound at a time.

1. To experience that layering—a natural soundscape, go somewhere new (a coffee shop, a park, an industrial site, a busy street, a wooded area). Bring a notebook.

2. Focus on listening to the scene, not watching the activity around you, and try to identify every sound you hear. Make a list of the sounds.

3. Try to think of a scene from a play or a situation into which those sounds might fit.

Fig. 3-22—SIU Theatre 101 Student Production Team Collaborating

Exercise #31

A Group Exercise on Design Collaboration:

A Mock Production Meeting

This exercise will likely take two class meetings. The objective is to simulate the feeling and work of a production team collaborating.

Instructions: *Each person (or pair) will take on a design role, or if preferred (or if working alone), that of scenographer. (We recognize that we have not yet experienced the role of the director, so this will be an exercise in design collaboration. Later, we will offer another one that includes the entire production team.)*

Discuss a scene from a play you have read and then, together, first in words, then with visuals and sounds, etc., make decisions about how you would produce it in the context of the entire play. Go back and review the design section of this book. This exercise should include discussion—give and take, or collaboration.

For example, is there an image off which the entire design might be based? A metaphor around which all the designers might work? Is your production going to be realistic? Non-realistic? Why?

Each Production Team Member (or combination) is responsible for accomplishing and presenting the following:

▶ **Set & Properties Designer**—Reaction or emotion words, inspirational images, description of what the set looks like. Do a quick pen or pencil ground plan. What type of theatre stage is utilized? How does your work reflect the overall vision & concept for the production? Even though you are working on only one scene, the setting must either work for the entire play or set changes must be taken into account. Be sure to include properties in your design. How do set and props reinforce the play's theme(s)?

▶ **Lighting Designer**— Reaction or emotion words, inspirational images, description of lighting effects. What mood are you setting for this scene? For the play? What colors might you use? Direction(s)? Intensity? etc.? How can the qualities of light work to reinforce the play's message and enhance rather than contradict set and costumes? Be sure to remember practicals if there are any.

▶ **Costume Designer**— Reaction or emotion words, inspirational images, description of costumes. What are the characters wearing? Who are they? When in time are they? Remember to include line, color, silhouette. Choose appropriate accessories. Would the characters wear the same costumes throughout the show or would they change? Might just pieces or props be added to change effects? How?

▶ **Sound Designer**—What sounds or music might you use at top and bottom of the show? Are there special cues within the piece itself? Is natural sound involved? Music to underscore? A theme across the play? Are practical sounds important? How can the sound be layered or tracked? How does sound reinforce the play's mood or theme(s)?

Your work should be presented together, compiled as one neat set of papers and/or presented orally. It should be clear that all of the elements presented belong together in the same production.

Closing Thoughts

In this exploration we offer a view of the overlapping elements of scenography that indicates a wonderfully vivid, rich, and ever-expanding creative world. The scenographic imagination described here is one not only of inspiration and artistry but also one of intellect and research. No matter what approach someone takes to execute a design, reading a play remains the key to unlocking the potential of any written text. The following exploration into the performer, director, and production dramaturg will provide another interesting view of how a written text is translated from page to stage. As you can see from the overlapping exercises for each design area–Set, Properties, Costume, Lighting, and Sound–in addition to their work on play analysis, designers all seek visual (and often aural) inspiration. Vital to the theatrical process is that, together with the director, they work jointly to put across a unified production: they collaborate. The production team generally meets on a regular basis, often weekly. Through sharing their research and imagery and discussing the overall vision and concept for the production, they make decisions.

For Further Exploration

American Theatre Wing. "Crafting Worlds: Theatrical Design." *Working in the Theatre.* American Theatre Wing. August 2013. Web.

American Theatre Wing. "Sound Designer." *In the Wings.* American Theatre Wing. August 2013. Web.

Jane Collins and Andrew Nisbet, eds. *Theatre and Performance Design: A Reader in Scenography* (London and New York: Routledge, 2010). Print.

Ellen E. Jones. *A Practical Guide to Greener Theatre: Introduce Sustainability Into Your Productions* (New York and London: Focal Press, 2014). Print.

Darwin Reid Payne. *The Scenographic Imagination, 3rd Edition* (Carbondale, IL: SIU Press, 1993). Print.

Rob Roznowski and Kirk Domer. *Collaboration in Theatre: A Practical Guide for Designers and Directors* (New York: Palgrave Macmillan, 2009). Print.

EXPLORATION FOUR

Performer, Director &
Production Dramaturg

*Inside every good play lives a question. A great play asks questions
that endure through time. We enact plays in order to remember
relevant questions; we remember questions in our bodies and the
perceptions take place in real time and space.*

—Anne Bogart, *A Director Prepares*, 21.

IMMERSION #4
Being Present in the Moment

Performers strive to stay engaged as they act their roles.

While they are delivering memorized lines, they have worked long and hard to
make these lines so accessible that they scarcely have to think about them. What
becomes more important is being present in the moment, awake and aware of what
is happening to and around them. This exercise makes us see how often we drift
from the present and start thinking about the past or the future. With practice, we
can become better able to stay in the moment both onstage and offstage.

NOTE: This is NOT a performance. It works best when everyone does it at the
same time. This way, individuals focus on their own execution of the exercise, and
the instructor can observe, commenting on the class's work as a whole.

Instructions: *Assume a comfortable position, eyes open. Make observations of your surroundings, **in the present tense**. State these observations aloud. Keep going as long as
you can without lapsing into past or future tense. When you say something that has to do
with the past or the future, stop and begin again.*

Example:

> *"I am working at my laptop. I feel my fingers on the keys. The screen is
> bright. My calendar icon keeps popping up for some reason. It is red. The
> other icons are lined up across the bottom of my screen. I am wearing black
> shorts and a black and white top. I have two rings on my left hand. I wonder
> what time it is." STOP. BEGIN AGAIN.*

The performer, of course, is the most visible member of any live performance event. S/he stands before watchers, appearing both natural and artificial all at once—natural because the performance is believable and artificial because watchers know that the person before them is in a designed costume, illuminated by designed lights, following a blueprint crafted by a writer, and moving about the space in ways a director has developed with them. During the rehearsal process, the director and dramaturg work diligently behind the scenes to maintain a sense of unity and cohesive storytelling so that the performer can look and sound his or her best onstage. In this exploration we examine the importance of the performer-director-dramaturg creative triangle. In particular, we point to ways in which questions about the world around us influence how a written text might move from the page to the stage.

The Performer (aka Actor)

For over two thousand years historians, practitioners, and theorists have tried to define "performance" and "performing." Though the root of both is found in the Greek word **mimesis** (mimicry), differing ideas on these topics have emerged, offering us a variety of ways to think about the artistry and craft of being a performer. There have been debates over the years about the best ways for performers to prepare for live performance. One school of thought insists that an "inside-out" approach provides spectators with the most believable portrayals. With the "inside-out" approach a performer researches the written text to enter the mind of his or her character. In this case the performer looks for clues to the goals and desires of his or her character and lets those drive choices in rehearsal. Conversely, another school of thought insists that an "outside-in" approach is the best way to prepare. With the "outside-in" approach the performer first imagines how the character might walk, talk, and gesture and then considers how those elements influence choices. So, which one of these is better? With over two thousand years of history to look at, we can honestly say neither is better nor worse than the other. In fact, a balance of each approach is probably most effective in preparing a character. The effectiveness of any approach to preparing for a role depends mostly on which way makes the performer feel confident in his or her choices. Furthermore, some roles simply call out for more of one or the other approach. Ultimately, every role requires physical, emotional, mental, and spiritual dimensions in order to believably live in the designed setting that creates the visual world of the play on stage.

The Inside-Out Approach to Acting

Ever since famous Russian actor-director Konstantin Stanislavski, collaborator Vladimir Ivanovich Nemirovich-Danchenko, and the Moscow Art Theatre came to North America to perform in the 1920s, the inside-out approach has maintained popularity. Stanislavski argues that the work of a performer is to create an "inner life" by basing performance choices on the personal history of a character as found in the given circumstances of the written text. These givens allow a performer to imagine him/herself in the same physical, emotional, mental, and spiritual life as the character they are portraying. This concept is known as the "**Magic If**." With this "what if" information, a performer can then figure out the character's **objectives**—the wants and needs of a character from a super-objective down to a minute-by-minute, even a second-by-second, objective known as a **beat**. This analysis allows the performer to derive consistency and an overall goal, which is often called a **through line of action**.

Since this is a lot of information to keep filed away during rehearsals, Stanislavski recommends actors score their texts by writing down the results of all analysis and imaginative choices, breaking them into workable units. These notations are of further use when thinking of **endowment**, when the performer must, for example, use props that are not the real objects (for example, iced tea instead of whiskey) or give the effect of being outside when everyone knows that they are

Exercise #32
What does my character want?

Freely adapted from Robert Cohen's *Acting Power*

Just like real people, characters have wants and desires, and they try to attain them. In attempting to get what s/he wants a character uses a variety of tactics.

Instructions: *Working in pairs, decide who will be "Character A" and who will be "Character B." Later, you will switch roles. You do not need to assume any particular roles or establish any relationship between your two characters. Character A determines something s/he wants from Character B. Character A may use only the word "Please" in communicating; Character B, for the time being, may only say, "No." Character A uses different tones of voice and physical gestures, repeatedly asking, "Please." Character B responds with, "No" until s/he finds Character A believable and sincere. Then Character B may respond with, "Yes." Swap roles.*

To avoid self-consciousness or a sense of performing, students (in pairs) may conduct this exercise all at the same time, with the instructor observing.

Exercise #33
The Silent Screen

Watching other actors is helpful in understanding and appreciating objectives and tactics they use to achieve those objectives. An actor's attempt to attain a goal or meet an objective can be observed without words. Find a "high stakes" scene– one where you know that a character wants something very badly– on a *YouTube* clip or DVD. Cue up the scene, but turn the sound off. Watch how the actor attempts to get what s/he wants. What are their facial expressions? How does their body move? Do they lean in toward another character? Turn their back and walk away?

---

inside, on a stage, or looking through an onstage window. Closely related to endowment is **sensory recall**, which is when a performer uses the five senses to awaken personal memories of both physical circumstances and sensations already experienced in his/her life.

Beyond sensations, performers often work with **emotional recall**. Emotional recall involves remembering a moment of a particular feeling from a past circumstance and then focusing an aspect of it on what the character is going through, as in sensory recall. Emotional recall, however, must be approached with great care. Choosing a moment that we have not yet worked through in our real life can result in an onslaught of uncontrollable emotion. Theatre should never be

---

Exercise #34
Endowment One—25 Ways to Use a Cube

This exercise is like the "Props" exercise on the TV show "Whose Line is It, Anyway?" It works best in two groups—observers and participants, but it may be done alone.

Participants each use a traditional rehearsal cube or plain chair. Their task is to use the cube in unusual ways, as if it were something other than a cube. In other words, they endow the cube with properties that make it recognizable as something else. For example, one might look at the cube as if one were watching television, or put an imaginary plate into the cube's opening as if it were a microwave, etc. Observers watch and comment on the variety of ways in which the cubes were used. Then the groups swap.

The instructor or a student calls out, "One, two, etc." possibly all the way to "Twenty-five" as participants transform their cubes into other objects, creating a fleeting situation or circumstance.

confused with therapy any more than the stage should be considered as "real life."

Stanislavski is not the first and only person to suggest that an inside-out approach might lead to a more believable experience for the audience. He is, though, the first to articulate such ideas in a systematic way, suggesting that attention to motivation of choices is the key to success in live performance. "The System" or "The Method" and its derivatives keep a performer from playing to spectators while keeping him or her "being" or "living" within a character.

In many productions, the setting requires that performers live in a world of the play that might be very hot, even a tropical environment. Recalling how we react to extreme heat allows us as actors to personalize our character and to incorporate reactions that are more believable than simply fanning madly. Think about how silly it would look to watch a group of characters sitting on or around a New Orleans porch all fanning themselves in unison! Localizing the place where the heat is most intense rehearses us for moments in production in which a character might get burned, for example. In a production, one actress needed to react to scalding hot spare ribs thrown against her bare back. She recalled when she had set the temperature in her shower too hot and burned herself.

Types of Gesture

Functional: Achieves a specific purpose like combing hair or scratching a bug bite

Conventional: Culturally-based replacements of words such as shaking head "yes" or "no"

Social: Culturally-based rituals of communication like "flipping the bird" or waving "hi"

Habitual: Repetitious, unconscious routine(s) such as licking lips, biting nails, or tapping foot

Emotional: Replacement for words when they are not enough (like smooching or a bear hug)

Ghost: Non-verbalized expression of an internal state, like wringing hands or biting nails

Fig. 4.1—Types of Gesture

Exercise #35
Sensory Recall

This exercise focuses specifically on how you might utilize sense memory in a particular moment in production. You may be guided through this exercise as a group, or you may work though it on your own, individually.

HEAT and COLD

Close your eyes and remember a time when you were hot. You may have been at the beach or at a pool. Perhaps you just came off the field, court, or track at an athletic event. Maybe you were walking down a busy street in a big city. Wherever you were, start by remembering all of the circumstances, then focus on the feeling of being entirely too warm. When you get too hot, where do you feel it most? If you have long hair, then do you feel it most at the back of your neck? Do you sweat heavily? Do the palms of your hands get moist? Your feet? How about your forehead? Zero in on where you feel the most warm, and focus there. After "localizing" the place(s) where you feel the most hot—and only after your recollection has made you feel warm—react to that feeling. You may lift the hair off the back of your neck. You might wipe your brow, etc.

Repeat the exercise using extreme cold. Again, recall a situation in its entirety, then localize and focus on where you feel cold the most—Toes? Hands? How about your nose?

Exercise #36
Endowment Two—The Senses

Taste: Drink a glass of water as if it were milk, your favorite soft drink, cough syrup. Remember how each liquid tastes. If it is carbonated, for example, then how does that feel?

Smell: Smell an artificial flower as if it were a rose, before moving on to some other kind of flower. Use an empty bottle and smell it as if it were whiskey, rubbing alcohol, hot chocolate, coffee.

Sight: Look out an imaginary window and see a beach, a thunderstorm, sunshine, a beautiful garden. Take your time and enjoy—relish—each detail of the scene you imagine.

Touch: Sit on a rehearsal cube or plain chair. Endow it with the properties of a "cushy" couch, a classroom chair, a recliner.

Sound: Close your eyes and just listen to the sounds around you. Now, try to hear the wind, rain, traffic, children on a playground.

The Outside-In Approach to Acting

We should note that Stanislavski never excluded the need to develop a character via external considerations. As a trained singer, he knew all too well that attention to technical details of voice, diction, and movement were important in communicating emotional and spiritual states. In fact, by the end of his career he had changed his mind on the usefulness of sensory recall, replacing it with a focus on truthfulness of physical actions as a way to avoid too much stewing in emotions. This shift in thought is the impetus for many twentieth century investigations of outside-in approaches to performance.

Michael Chekhov, nephew of Russian writer Anton Chekhov, is one of the pioneers of outside-in approaches in the twentieth century. Interestingly, Stanislavski considered him both an ideal pupil and a brilliant performer. For Chekhov, the approach to believability is tied to imagination, feelings, atmosphere, and gesture rather than strict adherence to "inner life" of a character/persona. Accordingly he devised a series of imaginative methods that explore connections between the body and the mind. With this psychophysical approach, a performer is trained in a variety of daily movements and principles that can bring about sensations and emotions in order to create an "inner event." This event creation and the ability to bring it to bear in live performance

Exercise #37
Fashion Photographer

Large group activity (may be conducted in smaller groups, with observers)

Participants cross the room on a diagonal as if it were a "runway" and they were fashion models. The instructor or designated student calls out emotions such as "Angry," "Ecstatic," "Grieving." When participants hear the emotion named, they freeze, assuming facial expressions and poses appropriate for the emotion.

Exercise #38
Walking the Walk

Large group activity (may be conducted in smaller groups, with observers)

To begin, slips of paper with particular character types listed on them are distributed to the class (i.e., model, librarian, tourist, teacher, priest). The group prepares to cross the floor, one by one, single file on a diagonal. As each person crosses, others observe and guess the identity of the walker. No talking. No props. Participants must convey their character through physical movement alone.

is what Chekhov identifies as the "Creative Individuality" of the performer, which has no direct connection to his or her emotional recall or images. **Creative Individuality** attempts to support a union between performer and character without the ego of the performer getting in the way, which he believes occurs with the inside-out approach (especially in the US).

Anne Bogart and Tina Landau developed another outside-in approach often referred to as *Viewpoints*. Drawing on elements of dance—particularly when thinking of time and space—Bogart and Landau

---

Viewpoints of Time

Tempo: How fast or slow movement occurs

Duration: How long movement(s) is/are sustained

Kinesthetic response: Spontaneous reaction to motion

Repetition: Internal or external repeating

Viewpoints of Space

Shape: Outline of the body or bodies

Gesture: A behavioral or expressive movement of the body

Architecture: Awareness of how the physical environment affects movement

Spatial relationship: Distance between things on stage

Topography: The landscape, floor plan, or overall design

Vocal Viewpoints

Pitch: Frequency of a vocalization

Dynamic: How loud or soft a vocalization is

Acceleration/Deceleration: How fast or slow a vocalization is delivered

Silence: The absence of vocalization, perhaps filled by gesture

Timbre: Quality of a vocalization

Fig. 4-2—Viewpoints of Time, Space, and Voice

devised nine physical "viewpoints" and five vocal "viewpoints" as a way not only to train performers but also to create visually dynamic movement for live performance. Bogart and Landau argue that training in and rehearsing these viewpoints is not only a physical technique for working outside-in but also an overall aesthetic approach to live theatre. They also insist that this approach is necessary because the Americanized version of Stanislavski's inside-out "System" is too confining. By thinking about time and space a performer is not limited in his or her character choices as they might be if only considering "inner life" as defined by the written text.

Basic awareness of body and mind is needed in either the inside-out approach or outside-in approach. This awareness often comes from exercises that relax both physical and psychological tensions and open the performer up to a clearer state of receptivity when building a character. It is also important to develop a sense of a bodily core, known as **centering**. It is from this center that all movement impulses emerge.

Another good habit to develop is a sense of play. Somewhere between our formative years and reaching college-age, many of us lose a sense of imagination and creativity. Since these are the foundation

Exercise #39
Engaging the Viewpoints

This engagement focuses on the Viewpoints of Topography (Space), Tempo (Time), and Acceleration/Deceleration (Vocal). Make sure that the performance of these Viewpoints is done with a soft focus so that you remain aware of your surroundings in their entirety.

1. Begin by walking about the room at the speed you would usually walk.
2. After a minute or so, all persons with blue eyes should begin to walk quickly.
3. After a minute or so of that, all persons with green eyes should walk in slow motion.
4. Pause. Talk about what it felt like to go quickly, in slow motion, or stay usual speed (Tempo).
5. Draw a simple grid pattern on the board. This is what everyone will now follow as they walk (Topography).
6. Combine the Tempo Viewpoint as described above with the Topography Viewpoint just drawn.
7. Pause. Now add in the phrase "I like walking quickly/slowly/normally" to match the tempo at which the topography it traversed (Vocal Acceleration/Deceleration).
8. Stop. Break into small groups.
9. Randomly choose an adjective (or have one assigned to you) that is relevant to a character from a play you have recently read (i.e. Drunken, Saddened, Enraptured).
10. As a group, develop and then perform the Viewpoints of Topography, Tempo, and Acceleration/Deceleration that match the character attribute/adjective.

Performance Ingredients

Relationship: A way of defining what a person or object means to a character

Objective: What a character wants

Obstacle: Something or someone in the way of an objective

Strategy: The plan to get around the obstacle to reach the objective

Tactics: Specific maneuvers within the overall strategy

Text: Things that are said (lines)

Subtext: Also known as interior monologue; things that are not said in the script

Evaluation: Reflecting on how well the overall plan is going

Beats: Shifts in scene, plan or objective

Being: Living in the character and not on top of the character

Fig. 4-3—Ten Performance Ingredients for Performers to Consider

Exercise #40
Roll Down

This can be a group or individual exercise, and is a common one that can be done with variations. It works on centering.

Participants stand, balanced evenly, with a comfortable space between their feet. Slowly, beginning by dropping their heads to their chin, they begin to roll their bodies down, toward the floor. The feeling should be that of moving down slowly, vertebra by vertebra. Stomach muscles should contract, as if a fist were pressing against the stomach, but not to the point of discomfort. Arms should dangle down (knees may be slightly bent), gradually touching the floor. Participants should rest in this position, then begin to reverse the process and roll up. The head should come to rest—not jerk up—and rest atop the body, aligned nicely. Repeat.

After completing the roll down a few times, participants should be centered, relaxed, and, at the same time, ready to move.

Exercise #41
Walking with Memory

Created by Becca Worley

Although this was designed as a group activity, it may be executed alone. It can be executed with two groups, one watching and the other moving, then reversing roles.

Instructions:

As you walk in space as yourself, with others, consider the following questions:

▶ What is your leading center? How does the rest of your body respond/follow?

▶ What is your natural tempo/rhythm? What patterns do you follow (topography)?

▶ Where do you look? What is your breathing pattern?

Now, change your center. How does the rest of your body adjust? Tempo/rhythm? Topography? Eye contact? Breath? What images come to mind (character types, abstract images, scenarios, etc.)? What emotions do you feel?

Next try walking ONLY in straight lines & angles, then ONLY in curves & circles.

Allow every part of your body to inhabit the shapes (angles/curves). How does your breathing pattern change? How does your tempo/rhythm change? How do you adjust as you encounter others in the space? What emotions do you feel? What images come to mind? How do your adjust or respond when half of the group walks in straight lines and angles, the other half in curves? Physically? Emotionally?

Relax and sit. Take a moment to think of a memory. This should be not only a strong memory but also one that you are ready to think about in detail. It can be happy, sad, serious, etc. but it should be a memory about a person. Where/When does this memory take place? Is it in a specific environment or is it a more generalized location (home town, school, etc.) Is it in a specific period of your life? A moment, a day, a general time period (when you were little, during middle school, etc.)? Who was the person you remember? What did/do they mean to you? If this memory was a color, smell, texture then what would it be? When you have the memory firmly in your mind, begin moving through the space. Allow that memory to fully take over your body as you walk. What is your leading center now? What is your tempo-rhythm? What is your walking pattern? (Imagine your feet are leaving the color of your memory imprinted on the stage as you walk.*) What happens with your breath?

What did you discover about your own body/mind/breath connection? How did these things change as you moved through leading centers, shapes, and memories? How can this be used in warm-ups before rehearsals? Before a performance?

*To more fully illustrate, use butcher block paper or cardboard on the floor and washable tempera paints on your feet and trace the topographies.

of performance, an actor must be able to freely imagine and create a character.

Auditioning and Rehearsing

Auditioning is the primary way that a performer earns a job. It may take one time to land a role or it may take hundreds of times in a year to land one role. If a performer is lucky, then one audition will earn them a spot with a company for nine months or at least for a summer. In an **audition** a performer tries to show a director that he or she has the physical, emotional, and vocal range needed for a particular role(s). A **prepared audition** is one where the performer memorizes and stages one or two minutes of material that showcases his or her best skills. Often performers will have ten or twelve different pieces drawn from classic, modern, and contemporary texts ready for any type of audition. Some of these will have heightened language, some will be comedy, and some pieces may even be in a foreign language. A performer may also have eight or ten bars of music ready and a few dance steps to go with them. A **cold reading audition** is just like it sounds in that it is an audition where a performer comes into the process without the opportunity to prepare a piece. Directors frequently use this audition to put performers on the spot to see how flexible they are vocally, physically, and imaginatively. Once hired, rehearsing takes over the life of a performer. Whether one week or eight weeks long, **rehearsals** are the time where performers learn lines, when and where to move (blocking), and

---

Broad Types of Rehearsals

Read Through: A time when the script is read out loud by the cast with the director listening

Blocking: A time when the director creates a traffic pattern and relationships using balance and composition

Unit: A time when the director works with performers on small portions of the script in order to polish and perfect character relationships, stage pictures, and storytelling

Run Through: A time when the performers put a script "on its feet" so the director can see what it looks and sounds like from beginning to end

Dress-Technical: A time when scenographic elements are married to performer choices in hopes of refining both so that a unified production emerges by opening night

---

Fig. 4-4—Types of Rehearsals

other stage business while building a character. As a daily process, a rehearsal can provide a repetitive, structured environment for performers to experiment, discover, and choose how they want to present a character. During this time directors often coach performers on timing of line delivery, give them basic blocking ideas, and generally support the investigations of a performer. The performance is the reason why performers are attracted to live theatre and performance. All the work of rehearsals comes to bear when on display before spectators. What cannot be prepared for are the coughs, laughs, tears, cell phone rings, and the like that watchers might "add" to the liver performance experience. Through it all a skilled performer can maintain a sense of being and presence. This is what makes theatre and live performance unique from film and television.

The Director and Directing

Directing is not new to the history of Western theatre. Ancient Greek playwrights and later Elizabethan-era writers like William Shakespeare, directed their own plays. What is relatively new is the notion of a single person, who is not the writer, known as the **director**—a person dedicated to the overall organization and orchestration of production elements, from script selection to design choices, from assisting performers in building a character to movement about the space. In the late nineteenth century Georg II, Duke of Saxe-Meiningen, supervised all aspects of production including rehearsals and design, striving for unity of production. Stanislavski continued to strive for unity and historical accuracy in his directing. Since then, the director has become a dominant force in live theatre.

The emergence of the director (and the trend toward Theatrical Realism in live theatre) coincided with both nineteenth-century social and political movements, like Marxism, and technological advances, like photography. Significant personalities including Karl Marx, Sigmund Freud, Charles Darwin, and Auguste Comte also had influence. Marx's writings about workers, the worker's state, and class struggle introduced the critique of Capitalism. Freud introduced the idea of inner psychology through his notions of the unconscious mind and repression. Darwin's *The Origin of the Species* precipitated the idea of evolution as scientific fact. French philosopher Comte created the discipline of sociology. These movements led to the expectation of Theatrical Realism—realistic settings, costumes, and psychologically motivated characters—on the part of watchers. Directors responded. Likewise, contemporary twentieth and twenty-first century directors have responded to rapid technological advances and scientific discoveries such as computers, the internet, and new media, pushing the role of the director beyond that of "custodian" of the playwright's printed work and into the realm of "author" of the production on stage.

Functions and Responsibilities

At its core directing is about both establishing a road map for a production team to follow and inspiring all the creative artists involved to walk the same path. This guiding vision, controlling idea, or overall point of view about how the written text should appear in live performance is what a director often uses to manage idea generation and joint thinking. Since each director and directing process is unique, we speak broadly about each and encourage you to further explore by researching specific directors and processes. In order to talk about the vast array of responsibilities of the contemporary director, we use three broad functions: artist, manager, and advocate.

Without knowing how the script works on paper, a director "as artist" will have a hard time devising a unified approach for a production on stage. In fact, it is from both analysis and interpretation that a director not only finds inspiration for his or her **directorial vision**—the idea or message to communicate to watchers—but also the way that s/he then corresponds with designers as they all begin their work together. This artistic work extends from the research/script interpretation phase into the rehearsal period in which s/he assists actors with their interpretation of their roles, "coaching" them and problem solving in

Fig. 4-5—A comparison of blocking for the same scene in *Rent*. The image on the left is from the SIU Carbondale production and the image above is from a Youngstown State production.

rehearsal and composing dynamic stage pictures that give spectators clues to relationships, focus, and mood/tone.

When thinking about dynamic stage pictures, directors use both triangles and levels to create focus (see Fig. 4-5). Try this in a scene between three people, two of them are close together in the upstage right area while the third is downstage left kneeling. The upstage performers are looking at the one downstage. Take a moment and draw this description, connecting the positions with lines so that a clear triangle can be seen. Now find three people and put this image "on its feet." What do you notice? Who is the most important? What is the relationship between the two upstage? How do you know these things even though no lines have been spoken? Moving persons about the stage and having them make a stage picture like those we just described is often referred to as **blocking**.

At the same time, the director "as manager" must cope with scheduling and calendar issues in addition to the overall logistics of bringing a piece from page to stage. Some of this managing can and does encompass leading discussions in production meetings to deciding which scenes need work and how many scenes to rehearse each day. It is also during this time that director-as-artist works also as director-as-manager to make sure that all design elements are communicating similar ideas.

It is vital to remember that live theatre productions are not simply reproductions of past performances or replicas of the stage directions printed on the page. It is in determining a vision and/or concept where

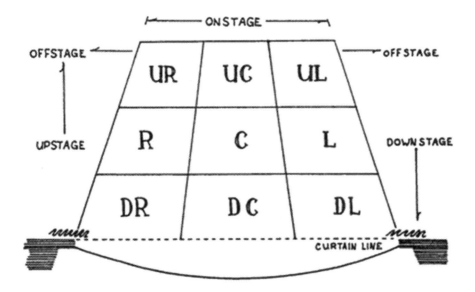

Fig. 4-6—The Geography of the Proscenium Stage

Exercise #42
Directorial Vision & Concept

Adapted from exercises created by Thomas Michael Campbell

Think of vision as the "what"—the most important or compelling idea/theme left in the director's mind after reading the play—what the director feels the play is about, the idea s/he wants to express—what the production will do. Think of concept as the "how"—the plan or the strongest way(s) to communicate the director's vision and set a mood for the production—how the vision will be realized. So, **vision** is the idea that drives a production and the message you want your audience to walk away with, while the **concept** is the way(s) the idea is expressed in the production.

Working individually or in small groups, conduct the following exercise and then share answers in large group discussion. You will determine visions and concepts for the following play.

THE PLAY:

This story is about a young girl (Little Red) on her way to take care of her sickly grandmother. While traveling she is confronted by a dark and manipulative character, and he tricks the young girl into revealing her destination. Upon arriving at her grandmother's home, she discovers the evil man has "replaced" her grandmother. Now she must take action to save her own life and uncover the fate of her beloved grandmother.

What about this story appeals to you?

▶ What is the central conflict?

▶ How does this (or might this) relate to current cultural/social issues?

▶ What message do you want to tell the audiences who come to see this production?

▶ If this story were a color, then what would it be? If it were a sound? A flavor?

▶ What mood or tone does this story establish?

▶ When and where do you see this story taking place?

These leading questions point you toward creating a vision for a production. Now, you can begin to flesh out your concept:

What does the "Big-Bad Wolf" look like in your mind (what is the first image that "pops" into your head)?

▶ Describe her/his style of dress (i.e. "shabby," "shaggy," "dirty," etc.).

▶ What does her/his voice sound like (i.e. "scratchy," "silky," "loud," etc.)?

▶ What celebrity do you see playing her/him?

What does Little Red look like?

▶ Describe her/his style of dress.

▶ What does her/his voice sound like?

▶ What celebrity do you see playing her/him?

Describe Grandma's house from Little Red's perspective as she approaches.

By focusing on description, you have taken the vision you created above and "put it on its feet". You have addressed HOW the production might look—its concept.

the director "as advocate" can make a mark. Scripts do not have to be staged in their original forms or genres. A director, working with a production team, can offer unique script interpretations that retain the integrity of the text and yet are relevant for today's watchers. In this way the director is advocating both for the text and for the watcher coming to see the live performance.

This section has offered just a small sample of the types of both artistic and practical considerations directors make as they go about moving a script from page to stage. Directing is one of those crafts that cannot necessarily be taught, but must be learned. By this we mean

Exercise #43
Creating Stage Pictures

Small Group Activity with a Full Class Discussion

Materials needed: Copies of famous paintings showing at least three and no more than seven people; photographs of groups of people may be used.

In groups of four, no more than six, participants "stage" artwork, such as the famous painting of Washington Crossing the Delaware below. The groups' task is to stage their painting as accurately as possible—to reproduce it using live bodies.

Discussion: *If possible, then project each group's painting or photograph for the entire class to see. Discuss where our eyes are drawn as we look at the picture and at the recreation with live bodies. Like fine visual art, in finely staged productions our eyes move to where the director wants us to focus.*

Exercise #44
"The Focus is on _____."

Direct Focus: We look directly at someone because 1) they are elevated above everyone else; 2) they are moving; 3) they are isolated from everyone else—i.e., lying on the ground.

Indirect Focus: We look from one object or person to another until we reach the primary object of our attention. For example, one person looks at another person, who looks at the next person, etc. until we reach the last person, on whom we focus our attention.

Larger Group Activity—Two groups, participants, and observers

Materials: a few rehearsal cubes or plain chairs

Participants take their place in a performance area (may be on stage). They move around randomly, until the instructor or leader calls out, "The focus is on Mary." Mary then "takes focus" by rising above the others or lying down, and the group "gives" Mary the focus, using the principles stated above. Focus shifts from one participant to another. Discuss how focus was created. Stop and "freeze" stage pictures and take suggestions from observers to [re]focus. Groups then switch places.

"The Focus is on _____" enables participants to feel focus, to sense shifting focus in their bodies. Observers can witness first-hand how the director works with balance and composition to stage pictures.

---

that each directing project is so idiosyncratic that there really is no one way to be a director. Yet, someone must learn how to do it in order for what we have discussed to happen.

The Production Dramaturg

Still a relatively new position within US theatre, the dramaturg has been a defined role in theatre since at least the eighteenth century. While it is true that if you get ten dramaturgs in a room you will get twelve different definitions of what they do, for our purposes here we think of the **production dramaturg** as a story manager who works towards continuity by integrating research with doing, rehearsal work with outreach efforts, and solitary pursuits in the archive with the group pursuits of generating a unified production. **Production dramaturgy**, then, is the process of seeking continuity through this work. Historians tells us that "the dramaturg" seems to have taken prominence during the German Enlightenment when Gotthold Ephraim

Lessing began publishing essays on a variety of topics related to theatre and live performance. These 104 essays, published in 1769 as *Hamburg Dramaturgy*, promote Aristotelian elements of drama. Lessing's critical writings earn him the distinction of being called the "Father of Dramaturgy." From this point forward across Europe the dramaturg became an established role. As with the director, while the position was not always named, someone always performed the role of the dramaturg. What exactly is that role?

Basic Duties of the Dramaturg

Dramaturgs creatively collaborate on moving a script from page to stage. The tasks handled by dramaturgs are so varied and so idiosyncratic that we cannot provide a definitive list here, but we can point to common processes and procedures in use both in academic and professional theatre. Dramaturgs research background information on the scripts being produced to help directors and designers establish a vision and execute a concept. This information can include historical sources for the script (like a poem or war battle), a production history, art work, diaries, literary criticism, films, magazine and newspaper stories, or any other artifact that might have bearing on creative decision-making on the way to continuity. Inherent to the story management is the production dramaturg as advisor. In this capacity the production dramaturg not only suggests ideas for continuity but also offers ideas about translations, adaptations, and other script preparation needs. For example, a family and children's theatre is interested in producing a popular Christmas play but does not want it to be the same version they produced two years ago. The production dramaturg seeks out the original story, filmic versions of the piece, as well as other adaptations to prepare a script that has elements these existing versions do not. The production dramaturg frequently plays the role of educator in that they use the background information gathered and rehearsal ideas to generate all kinds of written material (broadly defined) that will assist watchers in appreciating the live performance. In the end, the production dramaturg often serves as historian, script reader/evaluator, translator or adaptor, director's assistant, in house critic, and sounding board all at once.

To fully execute these duties, the production dramaturg uses many of the same research tools that the directors and designers do, but they do so (when they can) much earlier in the process. The production dramaturg also negotiates early on how long they will remain attached to a certain production process, looking up terms and concepts, researching social customs, and providing performers, designers, and the director with requested information and images. For example, a production dramaturg freelances for a summer Shakespeare company in the

Midwest that produces two shows in repertory. It is decided that he will attend the first two weeks of rehearsals for each play, be away for a week, and then return for technical-dress rehearsals while remaining available by email for questions in between. It is also agreed that the production dramaturg will host a pre-show talk for a senior citizens group, write synopsis material for the website and program, and produce a program note that somehow links the two productions thematically so spectators can better appreciate why these two scripts were chosen to be produced side-by-side during the summer season.

"The Book"

One of the foremost ways that a production dramaturg collects, collates, and creates information is through the use of "The Book." This is the place to collect all of the material generated over the course of a production process. This notebook will change and evolve as the production process moves from pre-production work alone and then with the director, to rehearsal, and then into the production run. Material will be added, some may be deleted. In the end, this is often distilled into a production pack for use by creative-collaborators. As technology has advanced, the dramaturg has become able to accomplish many of her/his tasks electronically. Entire production books, resource packs, etc. are stored and disseminated to casts and production teams via the web. Daily communications transpire over email, social media, and e-gathering places like *Google Hangout*.

The pre-director phase of preparation is when a production dramaturg reads the script, generates ideas about the plot, and researches as we mentioned earlier in this section. S/he does this to get a sense of what other productions have done well and have done poorly, to get a handle on the socioeconomic context (given circumstances) from which the script first emerged, and to get a sense of the writer and his or her background. In doing so, the dramaturg prepares to offer ideas for innovation. One of the foremost responsibilities of this phase is to generate a glossary of terms and concepts. The purpose in doing so is twofold. First, it allows the production dramaturg to get intimately familiar with the script and its meanings so that responding to questions in the moment becomes easier. Second, it is meant to save time in rehearsals for the director, actors, and designers. Of course there will be terms and concepts that will still need to be looked up and researched, but having this "jump start" certainly streamlines the process. The script dictates both the length and depth of "The Gloss." That is, if the production dramaturg is working on a contemporary piece, then the terms and concepts to be researched will probably be drastically less than the list of terms and concepts to be researched for a Shakespeare script. Once contact with the director is made and basic ideas about

Riverside Theatre Shakespeare Festival
Romeo and Juliet Production Pack

Table of Contents

From the Director

Fig. 4-7—Dramaturgical Production Pack Table of Contents

the script are shared, the production dramaturg seeks out information and images that assist in refining concept. This information is added to the book and often referenced during rehearsals and production meetings. During rehearsals, the book also becomes a repository for continuity noted, production meeting minutes, and performer queries. By the time the production opens, the material from the book has been transformed into educational materials, a lobby display (if applicable), a program note and other written material, and perhaps pre-show and post-show discussions. Ideally, once the production is running, the production dramaturgy book becomes an archive of the live theatre event and its production process.

Before leaving this section we should note that almost everyone on the production team does some sort of dramaturgical research as they prepare themselves for rehearsals and then opening night. What makes the production dramaturg so unique is the fact they are asked to be the connection linking all creative areas to help ensure, as best they can, a sense of continuity.

Exercise #45
On Dramaturgy

Created by Thomas Michael Campbell

Individual or Small Group Exercise

The Dramaturg may join the production team and work with the Director as s/he comes to vision and concept, or the Dramaturg may join in a little later. In any case, the Dramaturg "gets behind" and supports the Director's vision and concept.

Consider revisiting/creating your vision and concept for "Little Red Riding Hood" (LRRH) in Exercise 42. Using the vision and concept you developed for the play adaptation of the story, or the vision and concept presented here, list sources where you could find visual or printed information that might help the director and designers realize the production on stage. When you consider places you might look, for example the internet or books, include the key words you would use in your search—i.e. "male domination."

In both your own visions and concepts, and in those below, notice key words that might push you to research specific concepts or images on the internet, in books, etc.

LRRH Vision

The approach for this production looks at the world of LRRH as male dominated. Little Red is a character that overcomes this dominance and a predator (the Wolf) who, at first, has power and is in control. Our approach to LRRH is one of personal realization, strength, and courage as Little Red comes to understand the necessity of critically examining the subjectivity of "truth" set forth by a male-dominated society. What is presented to us is not always what we believe it be, and this is a story of a woman who fights back against the dangers of blindly and naïvely accepting the world as is.

LRRH CONCEPT

This play is draped in flowing fabrics of dark, blood-reds, royal purples, and shimmering blacks. Light breaks through the canopy of the forest at intermittent points, casting odd, long, large shadows. In the light, items shine and sparkle, as if in a dream. Yet in the shadows, the sparkles become muted, like when a thunderstorm blots out the sun, because, in actuality, the dream is a nightmare. LRRH exists as a distorted fairy-tale where nothing is as it seems: the nice and kind appear broken, the vile appear strong and noble, the brave appear small, and it is these fallacies that we break down as the story progresses.

You may continue with this project and follow through by finding sources and images to discuss.

Exercise #46
On Production Dramaturgy

Use a short play text like "Trifles" or "The Sandbox" for this exercise, or any other you have read for class.

1. After reading the play, choose three visuals to hunt down (i.e., a picture of a 1900s farm kitchen).
2. Using sources such as *A History of Private Life* (5 vol., ed. Phillippe Arles and Georges Duby, Belknap/Harvard UP, 1992) or *The U.S.A.: Chronicle in Pictures* (Neil Wenborn, NY: Smithmark Publishing, 1991), find at least two images you might show a set designer.
3. Keep track of each step of your research process.
4. Share what you found.

Closing Thoughts

In this exploration we offer perspectives on how generative ideas emerge from the creative triangle of the actor, director, and production dramaturg. What we have described is, admittedly, only a small facet of the work done by each of these creative-collaborators. This said, the material offered gives you enough background to better appreciate, if not understand, the many ways that shared conversations amongst these three practitioners can lead to a polished, unified production. We next turn to consider the watching process and how to write about what is seen.

For Further Exploration

Steven Breese. *On Acting: A Handbook for Today's Unique American Actor* (Newburyport, MA: Focus Publishing, 2013). Print.

Lenora Inez Brown. *The Art of Dramaturgy: Transforming Critical Thought into Dramatic Action* (Newburyport, MA: Focus Publishing, 2011). Print.

Michael Chemers. *Ghost Light: An Introductory Handbook for Dramaturgy* (Carbondale IL: Southern Illinois University Press, 2010). Print.

Julie Felise Dubiner, Anne Fletcher, Scott R. Irelan. *The Process of Dramaturgy* (Newburyport, MA: Focus Publishing, 2010). Print.

Michael Wainstein. *Stage Directing: A Director's Itinerary* (Newburyport, MA: Focus Publishing, 2012). Print.

EXPLORATION FIVE

Seeing & Writing about Live Theatre

After some years in the job, inundated with invitations and greeted wherever they go by smiling press representatives, reviewers are apt to forget that managements value their comments mainly because they are published.

—Irving Wardle, *Theatre Criticism*, 6.

IMMERSION #5
Audience Etiquette

You have probably attended some sort of live performance event—a concert, dance recital, or a play. For this exercise, a film at a movie theatre works. In fact, any place where a group of people gather to view and/or experience the same event, like church or a graduation ceremony, will suffice.

List the sorts of behaviors on the parts of others that have disrupted your enjoyment of the event or annoyed you—for example, someone seated near you repeatedly getting up to go out.

After you make your list, discuss it with others, and try to imagine what it would be like if everyone at the event behaved this way!

Attending a live theatrical performance involves its own set of **conventions** (rules or expectations). Watchers who are not prepared for seeing any type of live performance event can be distracting. Granted, expectations vary from event to event. The kind of behavior expected at a football game, for example, is different from that at live theatre. The theatre experience begins with your first encounter with the theatre building itself—whether that is a trip to the box office to purchase your tickets (or even interfacing with the venue's website to buy them online) or your entry to the lobby or when an usher directs you to your seat. Just as the **front-of-house personnel**, those who meet you at the door or get you to your seat, should treat you, the patron, with respect, answering any questions you might have, helping you exchange your tickets if you wish, directing you to the concession stand, restrooms, or gift shop if there is one, there are some guidelines you, the watcher, should follow in attending a production. Remember, a live theatre performance can be exciting. All of the people involved in the production work hard to be sure they give a great performance. Remember, too, that you the watcher are the fourth component to theatre-making (space, performer, idea, and *watchers*) so it is important that you work hard too.

One of the best ways to ensure a quality viewing experience is by arriving early for the performance, taking into account parking, getting to the actual performance venue, picking up the tickets, visiting the bathroom, and proceeding to the seating area. Sometimes if a patron does not pick up her/his reserved tickets ten minutes prior to the start of the first scene, then the theatre will release that reservation and sell the tickets to someone else on a waiting list. It is always a good idea to call and ask how early the doors will open. Arriving at your seat with extra time gives you the opportunity to peruse the program. If you are unavoidably detained and arrive late, then treat the box office staff, house manager, and ushers graciously. It is not their fault you are late. There are late-seating policies at every theatre, so let them work that process. Late-seating guidelines are established for the good of the audience, and sometimes they depend on the size and design of the performance space (intimate or huge) and on the duration of the performance (Are there act or scene breaks during which late-comers can be seated with less interruption?). This means that sometimes when you arrive late you may not be let in to your seat. In this case, simply exchange your ticket for another performance.

It is also a good idea to inquire in advance as to what kind of attire is preferred. For example, a ninety-nine seat theatre may indicate that business casual or urban casual are fine whereas the opening night of a Broadway performance may require some sort of more formal dress. Tourists attending outdoor theatre will dress differently from watchers going to a benefit performance of an opera. As you go about dressing for the event, it is also important to keep in mind allergies that watchers might have to ingredients in cologne or perfume. Two other considerations should be hairstyle and hat choice. Make sure that your hairstyle is not excessively tall or wide as it can block someone's view. Do not wear a hat into the seating area if at all possible. If it is necessary, then make sure it is not too wide or too tall so as to obscure the view of others.

There are some good housekeeping elements to attend to before the start of the performance. As mentioned above, make sure to visit the bathroom before you enter the seating area, especially if a cocktail hour has been part of pre-show activities. Once the performance begins, intermission is the next time this opportunity will be available without disturbing nearby watchers. If an audience member, including you, does have an emergency and needs to come or go to attend to it, then be quiet and careful as you exit. Have an usher indicate when a scene change occurs so that you can reenter with as little disruption as possible. Keep in mind, however, some productions have no scene breaks, and others do not have an intermission, so ask questions before the live performance starts if you anticipate needing to come and go.

All electronic communication devices should be shut off completely. Texting, talking, and taking out the device for any reason is distracting both to watchers and to performers alike (and just plain rude). There is no shortage of stories from Broadway where performers the likes of Hugh Jackman and Nathan Lane have stopped a performance to comment on the disrespectful behavior of someone texting (or phoning). On a technical level, some of the component parts of these devices can actually interfere with wireless control systems for lighting, sound, and the like. Even if a watcher is a medical doctor, the device can be left at the box office and an usher can offer notification of an emergency. If someone does forget to turn off an electronic device, then do not snarl at them or shout "Turn it off" in the dark as that is just as distracting and rude. It is also a good idea to put away any image-taking devices (video or still photograph cameras) as it is usually illegal for watchers to take pictures, moving or otherwise. Flashes distract performers and can even cause them to physically stumble so forget about using them until after the show if/when you meet the performers in the lobby.

Once the performance starts, try to sit still. Shifting, lifting your arms, foot tapping, and other such motions take attention away from the main event. Also resist the urge to begin talking to a neighbor. Whispering is still talking. Wait for intermission, or at least for loud applause or musical numbers to make any sort of comment.

Although some theatres now allow food and drink in the seating area, in general, neither of these has a place in a live theatre production. Go to lunch or dinner before you arrive so that you can engage fully with what you are watching. This said, some outdoor venues may encourage picnicking, so do some research. If there is a chance that something like a cough drop or piece of hard candy will be needed, then either unwrap them before the performance starts or wait for loud applause or a musical number to unwrap them.

If the seating area is close to (or even on) the performance space, then make sure not to clutter it with programs, coats, bags, or other articles of clothing. All are distractions and tripping hazards for performers.

Sometimes live theatre events hold the attention of watchers well and sometimes they do not. Sometimes watchers attend a production well rested and sometimes they do not. In either case, try not to fall asleep as the cast and crew can take it as an insult. Besides, snoring

will definitely disrupt other audience members' enjoyment of the production!

Singing along with musical numbers or scene change music is also
distracting and can provoke deep stares from other watchers. We had
an experience like this when watching a popular musical on Broadway.
Our seats were in a section filled with high school tour groups that obviously had played the cast album on the bus ride to the city. As much
as we wanted to fully engage the performance, the "singers" around us
often took attention away from the stage.

So many things to avoid, but what can watchers do? Engage fully
in the performance. Laugh when appropriate. Applaud when suitable.
Talk with other audience members about the experience at intermission and after the performance. Stay for the entire curtain call to show
appreciation for the work done by the cast and crew.

This introduction to watching live theatre has dealt exclusively
with audience expectations and behavior. Good watching is vital in
order for you to effectively evaluate a production. We need to pay attention to the performance in order to speak or write about it with any

Exercise #47
Performing the "Bad" Audience

Materials needed:

Small, individually wrapped hard candies

Programs (Available to download and print. Visit the title support page:
www.hackettpublishing.com/experiencing_theatre_worksheets)

Slips of paper assigning behavior:

▶ Dial someone's cell phone number and let it ring

▶ Stand up and leave the room, allowing the door to slam

▶ Tell someone they are in your seat and try to get them to move

▶ Eat the wrapped candy and crinkle the wrapper

▶ Crumple the program

▶ Whisper to the person next to you

▶ Take a flash picture with camera or cellphone

Instructions:

1. Hand out programs, slips of paper, and props as participants enter.
2. "Conduct" the cacophony of "badness" as if it is a symphony, bouncing from one
   sound to another while moving toward a climax.
3. Once set, have a select group get in front of the group and attempt to read over
   the noise.
4. Debrief the exercise and relate to the watching experience.

authority. We all have preferences, likes and dislikes, belief systems, and ideologies. However, these biases have no place in writing critically about performance. To critique performance (or any art form), we must practice aesthetic valuing and critical thinking.

Aesthetic Valuing and Critical Thinking

Aesthetic valuing and critical thinking are related. **Aesthetic valuing** ("aesthetic" defined roughly as the appreciation of beauty in art) has to do with determining the relative artistic (or in our case, theatrical) success of a piece, based on an evaluation that uses both the vocabulary of the discipline and the principles of the art. Asking us to "judge" the piece according to these and not from an individual gut response like "I liked it" or "I did not like it" is key. Personal taste need not be completely eliminated, but it must be supported with evidence from the text or production. Like aesthetic valuing, **critical thinking** invites us to observe, react, talk, and write using evidence-based reasoning, not just personal opinion. Critical thinking is necessary to success in any discipline or work place, and critical thinking can be increased through our aesthetic valuing of plays and productions.

Writers of Critique

While, to some extent, all watchers can offer commentary on an experience, both critics and reviewers are individuals who have dedicated themselves to writing about what they see (or read) with the purpose of informing a larger theatre community about that experience. Some writers of critique are on staff at a traditional publication or website while others are not. Some writers of critique are paid for their work while others are merely reimbursed for mileage and hotel stays. Some writers of critique work in higher education and analyze a play as a text, a play as performance, or both as a text and as a performance in order to better place the work in context for others. All writers of critique, though, are educated, intelligent, passionate people that not only

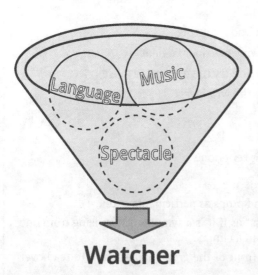

Fig. 5-1—The Important Elements of Drama when Watching

have the ability to conduct some sort of dramatic analysis but also possess the skill to recount that analysis in ways that are both interesting and engaging to a readership.

Those who write about plays and productions fall into two basic groups: 1) the critic and 2) the reviewer. For our purposes here, we call the person who has time to write longer critiques the **critic**. Published criticism varies in length and appears in many different types of venues—books, chapters in books, journal articles, and even peer-reviewed websites. We should also note that, in this case, "criticism" does not necessarily mean recounting errors or offering negative feedback. "Criticism" in this context indicates engagement in a thoughtful process of study and reflection, regarding to what extent elements work well, to what extent elements are confusing, and how or to what extent a production fits into the larger scope of theatre and performance history. Those who write opening night critiques of performances, then, generally for newspapers or sometimes magazines, we call **reviewers**. We will explore the type of work each does, focusing on similarities and differences meant to provide a sense of both styles of writing. We start, then, with a section on the person who writes what is often referred to as either dramatic or performance criticism.

The Critic

The critic is an individual who has time to prepare carefully written insights and findings about a production, for a specified theatre public. This is because, unlike the reviewer, who writes for a community of consumers (those who buy newspapers, for example), the critic often writes for a community of scholars (those who study). This means that a critic is usually not a journalist writing for the popular press but, rather, a person writing for a peer-reviewed publication (i.e., *Theatre Journal*) or at least a focused trade magazine (i.e., *American Theatre*). Student critics are often involved with the Kennedy Center American College Theatre Festival and, like you, perhaps, they find themselves writing response essays for classes. Although we separate writing about play texts (**dramatic criticism**) from writing about productions (**performance criticism**), professional critics (those who write books and articles and/or those who write performance responses) possess knowledge of a wide range of plays and often relate the play's literary qualities when they write about production. Because performance critics take time before sharing their conclusions, they often perform rigorous research regarding the play they have seen. At the core, then, a performance critic is someone who engages in critical thinking as they consider a particular watching experience, going over the choices made by writers, designers, directors, and the rest of the production team. When s/he finally writes up her/his findings, the ideas they

Important Elements of Criticism

1. Original viewpoint regarding topic or inventive approach to topic
2. Rigor of analysis
3. Case-making through use of evidence (either read or seen)
4. Clear organization of ideas
5. Readable style and syntax with appropriate grammar and punctuation

Fig. 5.2—Elements of Criticism

present usually provoke some sort of deeper creative thinking about form, style, genre, character, action, or any of the myriad facets of live theatre in production.

The performance critic is mostly concerned with the analysis of a particular watching experience in terms of its success or failure, not only to clearly interpret the play text as it appears in live performance but also to build on an existing production history of other times and places it has been performed. Remember, the professional critic may have years of experience from which to draw and is able to draw comparisons with other plays and productions so they are able to fit, or situate, the performance within a larger historical context. They do this by supporting assertions and conclusions with evidence drawn from a watching experience. What does that mean for you as a watcher?

The performance critic might look at a particular performer and compare her/his previous roles with the performance just watched, or s/he might compare the performer's work to other performers who have tackled the same role. A performance critic might also look at the work of the director and compare how s/he chose to approach this production versus a previous production. The performance critic may choose to write about design elements and designers, individually or as a group, in comparison to previous efforts or at least other designs of the same play in order to situate designs in a historical context. In the end, the better performance critics incorporate these comparisons into a final draft while still offering a clear sense of who, what, when, where, especially focusing on how and why. For someone to offer an analysis without adequate support of assertions goes against the significance of performance criticism. Because live performance events are fleeting in nature, the closing of a production marks a "death" of sorts, so the performance critic also preserves or archives the memory of the production with images and detailed description.

In the end, the critic focuses on a variety of areas directly related to the written text. This can include elements of form, use of a central image or guiding metaphor, representation of historical figures, biographical information from the writer's life, social or political events

---

Basic Performance Criticism Guidelines

1. Write in clear, active prose with no endnotes or footnotes.

2. Identify stage positions with the accepted stage geography terms.

3. Emphasize analysis of the production over plot summary (no summary needed for often produced or well-known plays and musicals).

4. Address production values vis-à-vis its historical moment, performers, director, design, style, or constituent watchers.

5. Consider production values or emphasize the importance of a live performance event culturally, politically, or contextually.

Fig. 5.3—Guidelines for Performance Criticism

that relate to the text, and so on. Criticism shapes (or at least refines) current understandings of theatre because it builds on existing scholarship by providing fresh insights or opinions.

One way to think of the role of the critic is to consider his or her task as part play analyst and part production dramaturg.

The Reviewer

The **reviewer** is a watcher who functions as either cheerleader or safety officer depending on the production they see. Some of them have an educational background in dramatic literature. Some are journalists assigned to the "arts beat." Regardless of vocational background, reviewers quickly develop a way to use the review they write as a vehicle to deliver a recommendation (good or bad) to other watchers. So, if a production is engaging, they use the review to share with potential audiences how and why they enjoyed the performance, most likely offering a positive recommendation (cheerleader). If a production is less appealing, then they use the review to warn potential watchers about pitfalls they might encounter when attending the piece (safety officer). Because reviewers often place themselves in the role of an "ideal spectator" who represents the tastes of a larger public, it is the reviewer's knowledge of her/his readership that most often guides not only the content but also the tone of the review. Given this approach, there is little objectivity inherent to a review.

Think for a moment about the last time you watched an episode of your favorite television show. Now recall how you described your viewing experience to a friend. What did you highlight as funny or engaging? Why? What was not so good about it? Why? Did you recommend they watch it? Why or why not? This is the type of work that a reviewer does. The better and more entertaining a reviewer is when writing up a viewing experience, the more people begin to take their advice seriously. Reviewers of repute are often those quoted in advertising

Exercise #48
Reading a Performance Review

Large group activity (instructor provides copies of performance reviews) OR individual exercise (to be completed on your own or as homework for class).

This exercise asks you to read, reflect upon, and analyze a published performance review in a journal. We suggest using *Theatre Journal.* Under no circumstances should you use a newspaper review of a play or musical.

Read through the article at least once, perhaps with an eye toward the author's thesis statement and topic sentences in each paragraph, before answering the following questions.

1. What are the author's main arguments?
2. On what aspects of production does the author focus? Directing? Acting? Design?
3. Does the author relate the production to the script as written? To other plays? By the same playwright? By others?
4. How does the author/reviewer situate the production? Historically? By style?
5. What new information about the play or production do you get from the performance review?

materials or play covers of a published version of the script. Three of the better-known reviewers in the United States are Chris Jones in Chicago, Charles McNulty in Los Angeles, and Ben Brantley in New York. Each has had the opportunity to be both cheerleader and safety officer for many productions. What distinguishes them from the thousands of other skilled reviewers is both their artistry and insight when writing up a watching experience and their large readerships beyond the theatre market in which they are located.

While many of you may not read a lot of theatre press, most of you are probably already familiar with the type of article a reviewer produces, especially if you look for recommendations on film and music selections to stream or download. Nevertheless, when thinking about the tone and style of a theatre review that might appear in a large publication like the *Chicago Tribune, The New York Times,* or even a small publication like a campus newspaper, it is important to keep in mind that the piece should work in much the same way that a book report does. That is, it should be something that stimulates interest (either positive or negative) in potential watchers by describing as much as possible about the viewing experience without revealing too much and becoming a "spoiler." Written on a tight deadline, theatre reviews are also often limited both in content and in word count (usually 500-1500 words). The idea is not to provide an exhaustive situating of the text in performance but rather to offer an immediate, first-person reaction

---

A Basic Model for Review Writing

Who, what, when, where, and why: Provide the given circumstances of the watching done.

Plot review and/or synopsis: Use events that are important to the review to fill potential watchers in on the story.

Acting and directing (and choreography if a musical): Reflect on stage pictures, character interactions, and the like; paying attention to those moments and images that hold attention and those that do not (and why).

Design elements: Reflect on lights, setting, costumes, sound, projections, and the like; pay attention to those moments and images that hold attention an those that do not (and why).

Reaction, opinion, and overall recommendation: Close with a final evaluation based on evidence provided in previous sections.

Fig. 5.4—A Model for Review Writing

to the experience. As such, what follows is a suggested starting point when attempting to write a review. Although we offer a five-paragraph model here to get you started, each reviewer and publication frequently work closely together to devise an appropriate approach.

Many reviewers open with basic *who, what, when, where, why* information. In this case *who* refers to the producing organization, *what* is the performance being watched, *when* is obviously the day and time the reviewer saw the production, *where* is the proper name of the theatre (and perhaps city), and *why* can cover whether it was opening night or if a special charity or performer was featured. The point of this paragraph is to clearly recount the given circumstances of the viewing. The next paragraph should offer potential watchers a **plot synopsis** that recounts elements of the sequence of events vital to the overall review. This serves two purposes. First, it may remind readers about the finer points of a play with which they are already familiar or saw years ago. Second, if watchers have never seen or read the play, then it offers them a nice window into the world of the performance. It is often good form to follow the synopsis with a discussion of acting and directing (and choreography if a musical). This should highlight strengths and weaknesses of either the entire ensemble or specific performers. The fourth paragraph should consider design elements, particularly in regards to how they either do or do not work together to effectively create a unified production.

The last paragraph is reserved, then, for reaction, opinion, or a parting recommendation based on the previous case-making in the review.

Review Pitfalls to Avoid

1. Censorship (über-safety officer)
2. Excessive cheerleading
3. Unjust war with the pen
4. Know-it-all tone and style
5. Restaging or redesigning the production (because writer is a frustrated artist)

Fig. 5.5—Review Pitfalls to Avoid

Put another way, this is the "Dear potential audience member, here is what I ultimately think and why you should/should not go see this production based on my experience" paragraph. This closing paragraph is particularly important in large theatre markets, like New York City, Chicago, or Vancouver, because a strong recommendation can mean a box office success while a poor review can lead to immediately closing the production in order to avoid losing too much money.

Given the weight that reviews can carry, there are some important aspects of writing and content ethical reviewers try to avoid (Fig. 5-5). One of the most important pitfalls to circumvent is censorship of any kind. It is not the job of a reviewer to object to content. This approach is taking the safety officer role a little too far. They should, however, write a warning to potential watchers if there is either strong language or adult themes that some might find objectionable. At the same time, a reviewer must be careful not to be an excessive cheerleader (think Cheri Oteri and Will Ferrell in the "Spartan Spirit" sketches on *Saturday Night Live*). If any reviewer stays too excited about everything they see, then they will lose the respect needed of their readership. Any production, even the best at Lincoln Center in New York, has places where watchers are drawn in and taken out of the live performance event. Report on that. Be honest. Reviewers must also try not to think of the pen as a sword and go about writing harsh, negative pieces that often kill off anything that they consider "bad theatre." When writing from this place of retribution, reviewers put themselves ahead of the taste of the larger theatre public. Reviewers need to consistently work hard to find a balance of good to go with the bad. Another pitfall reviewers should avoid is coming off as a know-it-all pontificator of all things great about theatrical production. If readers want a teacher to talk at them, then they will go to the local college or university and enroll in a course. Just as dangerous is the thwarted theatre artist who uses a review to share how *they* might direct, act, design, or otherwise better mount the production. This is neither helpful nor useful to potential watchers. Ultimately, crafting reviews takes continued practice

Exercise #49
Review Writing

PART I

1. Choose one of the plays you are studying.
2. Find at least three different reviews in major news publications (i.e., *The New York Times*, *Variety*).
3. Identify how the writer of each piece positively or negatively discusses the watching process.
4. Identify and list all of the positive remarks, noting phrasing choices.
5. Identify and list all of the negative remarks, noting phrasing choices.

PART II

1. Now that you have studied structure and flow, go see a live theatrical event with the purpose of writing a review.
2. With your production notes at the ready, begin by writing an opening paragraph that covers the name of the production, the producing group, the dates, etc.
3. Follow this with a paragraph that fills in the details of plot, story, and main idea.
4. Use the next paragraph to address strengths and weaknesses of technical elements.
5. Use the next paragraph to address strengths and weaknesses of performer choices.
6. Use the next paragraph to address strengths and weaknesses of director choices.
7. Close with original, thought-provoking conclusions, beliefs, opinions, or other revelations based on your watching experience.
8. Submit your review.

and study not unlike the work that playwrights do to make the pieces they write better.

Closing Thoughts

Writing about plays in performance (and writing about a play you have read) is an important part of the art-making that happens in live theatre. Though we have only scratched the proverbial surface here, we hope that you have a clearer impression as to why the reviewer, critic, and spectator are all valued members of the dialogue surrounding live theatre and its history.

For Further Exploration

American Theatre Critics Association. American Theatre Critics Association. ATCA, 2014. 6 May 2014. Web.

American Theatre Wing. "Theatre Journalism: Online and Off #399." *Working in the Theatre*. American Theatre Wing, May 2011. 9 January 2012. Web. Accessed via *YouTube* 7 May 2014.

Otis L. Guernsey, Jr. *Curtain Times: The New York Theatre 1965–1987* (NY: Applause, 2000). Print.

EXPLORATION SIX

Outreach

The pursuit of art and truth is the first requisite for serious theatre and it allows little room for self-serving social, financial, or political motivation. Nevertheless, people are motivated by different whys and it is a combination of whys that brings people to theatre projects.

—David M. Conte and Stephen Langley,
Theatre Management, 2.

IMMERSION #6
Outreach/Public Relations/Audience Development

Think of an event or cause that is important to you. It need not be of social or political concern. It can be as simple as a fund-raising event for a group to which you belong or an athletic event. You want to encourage more and different people to attend this event. Create the following:

- ▸ A catchy graphic that draws the eye and visually summarizes the event. (Describe this visual if you do not feel comfortable drawing.)
- ▸ A list of the kinds of new people you want to attend (members of another group or club, parents, etc.).
- ▸ Write one sentence that captures why people should attend this event.
- ▸ Think of at list one unique way in which you might reach this group.

"Outreach" is a comprehensive term that addresses the reciprocity between audience and event, the **audience-stage dialectic** (moment-to-moment communication between the two), and more. Outreach efforts encompass all activities that relate to bringing live theatre to more and different audience members. Most importantly, perhaps, it includes activities meant to build an audience of the future. Some of these activities include public relations ("PR"), marketing, education, community service, and even work that might be considered socio-political in nature. The fact that outreach efforts are designed to bring theatre to greater numbers of watchers with the least amount of resistance does not mean that all these efforts are offered free-of-charge. Even a not-for-profit company operates within a budget. Most companies and departments strive for a balance between selling tickets to those who can afford them and offering discounts, special events, volunteering at community centers or in schools, participating as a group in community benefits like walkathons, and other awareness-raising strategies.

"Events" are most likely as old as the notion of community itself. Evidence indicates that fifth century Athenian dramatic festivals were well attended, and the position of *archon*, or in contemporary parlance, "financial angel," was undoubtedly a coveted one. A sixteenth century production in Bourges, France with a cast of hundreds and a parade was a gigantic "plug" for Bourges's burgeoning textile industry. Royal patronage was important in the ages of both Shakespeare and Moliere. As with many of the job descriptions associated with theatrical production, "outreach" was accomplished by someone long before anyone ever had an official job title related to it.

Getting Organized

Before a theatre (professional, amateur, university, or other organization such as a community theatre association) can develop a successful outreach plan, the company needs both a clear and concise **mission statement** that responds to: What is the theatre's purpose? Why should it exist? For whom does it exist? It does so in order to fulfill a particular mission. For example, Chicago Dramatists is a company that nurtures new playwrights and offers them a forum for readings and production. In the same city, StageLeft Theatre also fosters new playwrights, but in 1988 the company expanded its mission to focus on developing and producing plays that offer, or at least elevate, debate on both political and social issues. The American Repertory Theatre (A.R.T.) at Harvard University has long held as its mission both producing new work and reimagining the classics. Recently the company "enhanced" its "core mission to expand the boundaries of theatre." The acclaimed Guthrie Theatre in Minneapolis states its mission: "By presenting both classical literature and new work from diverse cultures, the Guthrie illuminates the common humanity connecting Minnesota to the peoples of the world." Theatre Conspiracy in Vancouver, B.C. "creates theatrical events that activate discussion on vital contemporary themes in the international conversation." These few examples—and you can search the web for many more—suffice to illustrate the concept of mission or purpose. Check your theatre department or college/university website for information on its mission.

Understanding a producing organization's mission is vital to those in charge of selecting the company's season of plays and to those executing the many facets of outreach. Productions and outreach need to complement the organization's goals. Ways of cultivating new audiences for live theatre are not "one size fits all." What is successful for one company or theatre department will not necessarily work for another. Strategies that bring droves of people to one production will not always draw crowds for another event. Different groups of people, of course, are drawn to various productions. Strategically staged flash mobs might work for a musical that appeals to young people, for example, yet be inappropriate for a classic play meant to appeal to an older demographic of watchers.

The potential number and kinds of outreach projects knows no bounds. Large professional theatres often divide outreach activities into categories like "Education" and "Community Outreach," establishing particular offices to execute related tasks. Explore the websites for the theatre companies mentioned above and you find a wide array of outreach activities including classes, lectures, tours, and more.

Typically, a college or university theatre program is lucky to have a person designated for outreach, even if s/he holds other jobs as well. Take a moment and go online to look for some theatre organizational charts—or at least organizational roles—and see how "outreach" duties are handled at these theatres. This should reveal how many ways "reaching out" can and do occur.

Outreach is complicated, even limited, by budget and personnel. Unfortunately, the notion of "reaching out" is problematized, even compromised, by financial considerations that sometimes conflict with educational imperatives and humanistic ideals. By this we mean that while theatres (and college/university theatre departments) want to give both students and community members opportunities to collaborate on all kinds of performance events and to expose audiences to original, unusual, or seldom produced pieces, sometimes finances prohibit this from happening. If a theatre is dependent on box office revenue to support its programming, then a major consideration, sadly, becomes what theatre people call an issue of "butts in seats"—ticket sales. The necessity of selling tickets (and subscriptions) need not preclude good, honest, meaningful outreach.

In the end, outreach often takes plenty of imagination and ingenuity. A professional summer theatre recently provided community service to a local no-kill animal shelter in conjunction with a production that featured a dog. Before and after the performance, the theatre company allowed the shelter both to exhibit dogs that were up for adoption in the lobby and to accept donations. In addition to the rescue dog that starred in the show, a different dog was featured at each performance in a "dog catcher" scene. The shelter received numerous donations, several of their dogs were adopted, and apart from theatre personnel taking the time to organize this alliance, the outreach event did not cost the theatre company anything.

Public Relations/Publicity/Marketing

Most theatre companies include a Public Relations Department, the position of "PR Director," or, alternatively, Publicist. In this era of "spin," the phrase "public relations" takes on a negative connotation when, in fact, it merely refers to the office and personnel that interface with the public. Public Relations, no doubt, involves advertising and marketing, and regardless of who executes the tasks, someone: 1) creates a press release that advertises the play through "blurbs" or articles in newspapers, magazines, or trade journals; 2) designs posters for the performance event (or arranges for them to be created, for example, through a graphic arts department's students); 3) creates the program; and 4) generally fosters good will within the public for the particular performance and for the company at large.

As part of this process, a **press release** encourages the media (print, radio, and television, etc.) to contact the theatre for more information. It needs to be "short and sweet," provocative in the sense that it needs to make its audience desire more detailed information, and promote the event. The press release is written in the third person, like a news story. Essential information is presented in the first paragraph (title, venue, dates, times, cost, contact telephone number, website, etc.). The rest of the information is presented in order of decreasing importance. All of the information should fit on one page, typed. Generally the press release offers an attention grabbing title for readers (i.e. "Award winning!" or "One night only!"). More and more this type of media awareness-raising is being done with social media or other electronic forms of communication.

While press releases provide information on single events, other print matter forecasts the season at large (i.e. brochures, posters) and the company must maintain an active profile in other ways (i.e. website, Twitter). Just as a concise, specific mission statement serves as a vital "sound bite" or verbal profile of an organization, companies utilize **logos** (a mark or emblem commonly used to foster instant public

Exercise #50
Writing the Press Release

Think of an event or cause that is important to you. It need not be of social or political concern. It can be as simple as a fund-raising event for a group to which you belong or an athletic event. You want to encourage more and different people to attend this event.

Write a one page press release for this event.

Exercise #51
Creating a Logo

Now that you know a little bit more about publicity, re-design the logo you created for an event as outlined in the immersion at the outset of this chapter.

Share both your rationale and final product. If you do not feel comfortable drawing, then describe your logo. Discuss how your logo captures the attention of the particular audience you wish to gain.

recognition) for visual recognition and stay in the collective memory of the general public. Think of the ubiquitous "golden arches," Nike's "swoosh," or Ralph Lauren's polo figure on shirts. Similarly, the theatre companies referenced above have logos. Visit their websites again and take note of these visual representations. Logos are often developed for individual productions in similar ways to apparel logos, especially for professional productions in major cities. Yellow cat eyes against a black background constituted the logo for a long-running musical. A white half mask became synonymous with another world famous production. As these examples indicate, a logo needs to be simple, recognizable, and eye-catching in order for an audience to remember it and associate it with a specific show.

Audience Development

Audience demographics are important to a theatre in terms of retaining existing watchers while also targeting new audience members. College and university theatres in particular often serve two target audiences—a loyal group of older patrons who buy season tickets, and students. These audiences may, in fact, have competing tastes, making season selection even more difficult, and presenting the "total package" a conundrum for publicists. Imaginative marketing strategies must be developed to reach both groups. Sometimes seasons are created that have some events that target one group, with classic selections meant to address the tastes of the other. For example, new plays, experimental works, or plays that, for one reason or another, are educationally sound in teaching future practitioners, may not have broad-based appeal. These "experimental works" are sometimes offered to regular patrons of the larger venue at discounted rates to entice them to come. Often individual pieces are selected around a particular season theme, or a theme is created to encompass the plays selected. For example, a small theatre might use the notion of "Balancing Acts" to choose a season that includes plays in which the plot of each relates thematically to some sort of attempt to maintain equilibrium in tough times or challenging situations. Always cognizant of the need to reach out to more people and build an audience, the person in charge of group sales might notice thematic concerns in the performance events and contact members of various groups. For example, despite its message of warning to slumlords, a play about those same persons entertained people attending a major realtor convention in Boston. Fortuitously, during this same season, a dentist's conference provided a full house for the same theatre's production of a play that featured a dentist character.

In order to create the next generation of watchers, other modes of outreach are more important than those directly linked to marketing endeavors or quick-cash gimmicks. These outreach activities include and extend beyond the classroom. They take many forms, such as in-class exercises and assignments, pre-show lectures or demonstrations, talk-backs or panels, and visits to schools and the community. Again, responsibilities converge and overlap, depending upon the size of the theatre organization or department. Large theatre companies are divided into areas for community outreach, education, marketing and public relations, and dramaturgy. In the college or university setting, the tasks of personnel in these departments often rest on the shoulders of an individual faculty or staff member, assisted by students. Sometimes in academia, special events and lectures fall under the auspices of the university or college, and departments can apply for a slot and for funding. In professional, amateur, or academic theatre the community's greater calendar might provide opportunities for collaborations. For example, coordinating performances with Black History Month celebrations; aligning events with Women's History Month programming; featuring Gay, Lesbian, Bisexual, and Transgender awareness activities; Earth Day eco-performance, and so forth are all great calendar moments that can be used to make larger connections. Many college

Exercise #52
Targeting an Audience

You are the publicist or Public Relations Director for a small professional theatre company in the Midwest. Your theatre has decided to produce a piece that is set on the New England coast and deals with lobstermen!

▶ Consider what problems might arise in marketing this performance event to an audience many of whom have never seen the ocean.

▶ Consider what connections you might make between the subject matter of the piece and your "target audience."

and university departments as well as professional theatre companies participate in "V-Week" with productions or readings of material meant to empower women. Other examples include the reading of ancient Athenian anti-war dramas as part of a contemporary anti-war movement or the presentation of texts that deal with California's repeal of Proposition 8. These last events are world-wide efforts and illustrate how a single performance event can be socially conscious and fit within the context of global concerns.

Many theatres offer pre-show lectures and panels and/or post-show discussions with regularity. Pre-show discussion activities tend to point watchers toward salient thematic concerns in the piece they are about to watch or highlight aspects of the production itself. Some recent pre-show lecture discussions at a university include an English professor and a Theatre History professor looking at the world of a play about memories from their own disciplinary perspectives, illustrating how terminology is similar yet different across these two fields of study. A choreographer demonstrating particular movements and how they further plot progression was another offering for a movement-based play. Later in the year, a doctoral candidate discussed the "foul" language in a production utilizing charts and graphs to explain its use for an older audience that would be attending the same production as large groups of college students, for whom the play had great appeal. Another production found a music professor pointing toward recurrent musical motifs in a double-bill of one-act plays written by different authors as a way to link the two seemingly unrelated plays.

Post-show programming typically falls into two main categories: talk-backs with production team members (or, in the case of new works, with playwrights) and panel discussions that address thematic concerns and connect the piece with wider socio-political issues. The latter panel model might be held at a time other than immediately following the production when audience members may be in a rush. One

Exercise #53
Panel Discussion Planning

1. Choose a play or musical with which you are familiar.
2. Consider topics dealt with within the text.
3. Generate a list of potential participants for a post-show panel discussion and identify how their areas of expertise relate to the topic(s) you identified. Be interdisciplinary in your selections, because crossing disciplines draws a wider audience.

example of this is a panel comprised of psychologists, administrators, and counselors talking about sexual harassment to follow a college production that takes as its subject ambiguities in the actions of a college professor and his female student.

Another panel, held during Women's History Month, included women in aviation and supplemented a production piece that dealt with female flyer Jackie Cochran.

Collaborating with P-12 Educators

Educational outreach is a "two-way street." Students need to attend productions and feel comfortable in the theatrical venue, and theatre practitioners should travel to meet students in their own environments. Time and budgetary constraints make both of these modes of outreach difficult, and often, in college and university theatre, almost impossible.

Additionally, decisions must be made about what form outreach sessions will take, differentiating between **theatre for youth** (youth actively engaged in theatrical production, performing) and **children's theatre** (in which adults serve as actors, youth as watchers), as well as determining whether the programming will be directly connected to a performance event or manifest as a workshop (in creative drama, for example). The easiest educational outreach activity to manage is offering special student performances of suitable pieces. Advanced mailings to teachers may offer discounted ticket prices and announce designated performance times, and reservations can then be made. Student matinees are often accompanied by "meet the cast" sessions or other programming. Information on specifics of the productions can be sent to teachers who plan to attend with their students. Unlike the resource packets the production dramaturg prepares for the production team, these packets may include age-appropriate lesson plans and other suggested activities.

Another successful and manageable educational outreach program is a series of workshops and short readings or performances for

---

Exercise #54
Educational Outreach

1. Choose a play or musical with which you are familiar.
2. Research local schools to see for which age group the play or musical is appropriate.
3. Write a lesson plan that could be conducted during an average class session at a local school.

students, held at the theatre on a single weekend day. Students can be divided into groups and a rotation of workshops such as fight choreography with trained personnel, improvisation, acting, technical theatre, etc. can be conducted in separate spaces in the facility across the day. Lunch may be provided, and the entire group may gather at the event's conclusion, perhaps for awards. Theatre-in-the-schools programs are popular as well, but more difficult for academic theatres to schedule around their own classes. Some professional companies offer this sort of programming with regularity, bringing performances (often excerpts cut from pieces in production) and/or workshops into schools (look at About Face Theatre in Chicago). Other educational outreach activities might include in-service days for teachers, technical theatre consultations with schools purchasing equipment or renovating or building a facility, or even production assistance from a production dramaturg or choreographer.

Community Outreach

In addition to specific programming, community outreach, broadly speaking, relates to any interface between a theatre producing agency and the local or regional community or beyond. On the local level, of course, fostering a sense of good will between the company and those who inhabit its immediate environs is crucial to audience development, but more importantly, sincere community outreach demonstrates good citizenship on the part of the theatre. Sometimes community outreach relates thematically to the production season. Sometimes it simply demonstrates the theatre's willingness to participate in local "good works" like charity walks, benefits for other organizations, seasonal celebrations, and the like. Theatre-specific community outreach might entail providing lighting for a church group, offering a lecture at the public library, loaning equipment to a local community theatre, holding a benefit reading or performance for a social cause. The list is endless.

Exercise #55
Community Outreach

1. Research a professional theatre company's education department.
2. Analyze what sort of community outreach efforts they have.
3. Think about the plays or musicals you have read and make a list of which might be appropriate for such events.

The Bigger Picture

Sometimes a theatre company or college/university department is offered (or creates) an opportunity to join with other agencies or departments in a community celebration or for a common cause. The producing agency or theatre department may initiate plans for such an event or participate with a production or activity they already have scheduled. Colleges and universities often offer Orientations, First Year Experiences, or interdisciplinary or theme-oriented classes for which attendance at a theatrical production might be appropriate.

Many colleges and universities utilize theatre departments' improvisation groups to conduct orientation activities, sometimes based on social issues, or to lead team-building activities. Productions can also be utilized in this way. Those that deal with issues like sexual harassment on a college campus, for example, can be produced in conjunction with a First Year Program. Giant puppets created in design/tech classes at a university have appeared in the city's fall festival and Christmas parades. Since college and university campuses are often the sites for professional meetings and conferences, appropriate productions or staged readings can coincide with these events. Some of playwright Thornton Wilder's work was produced at the university that hosted the First International Thornton Wilder Conference. *Ragtime*, a musical about immigration and race issues in the US in the 1910s and 1920s, was staged in conjunction with the Peace History Society's international conference. Internet research calls forth numerous other examples. Several years ago, we were involved in planning a small on-campus conference in which our entire Department of Theatre became involved. This sort of city-wide, intra-departmental or interdisciplinary, campus-wide programming speaks to the vitality of theatre in relationship to community—but organizing such an event is a lot of work! Included here is the "Event Paradigm Chart" we created for an outreach initiative a few years ago (Fig. 6-1). We have utilized similar charts in planning subsequent integrations of productions with classes, guest artist visits, special lectures, and the like.

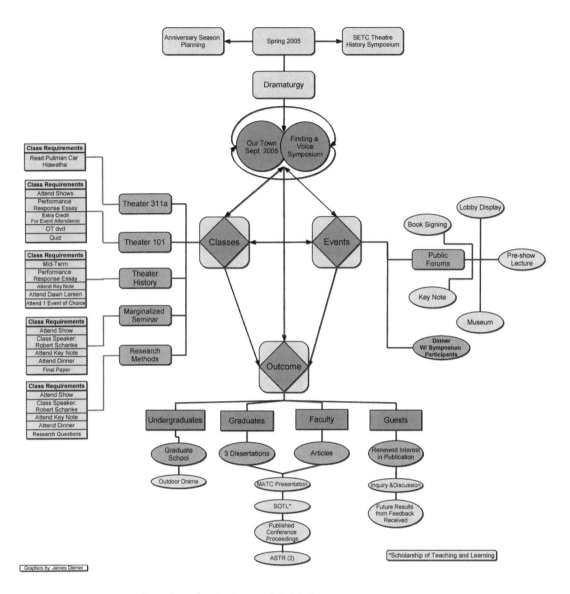

Fig. 6-1—An Event Paradigm Chart for An Outreach Initiative

Closing Thoughts

Making and maintaining a connection with other organizations, schools, the local community, and beyond strengthens the artistry of any theatre organization. The "different whys" referenced earlier in this Exploration or the bridge to the community-at-large that outreach activities attempt to build is all about a healthy exchange of ideas, perspectives, and information. Active engagement, care, and compassion are part and parcel of the humanity that lies at the core of theatrical production. These should be reflected in any and all outreach efforts no matter how big or small.

For Further Exploration

Joanne Scheff Bernstein. *Arts Marketing Insights: The Dynamics of Building and Retaining Performing Arts Audiences* (San Francisco: Jossey-Bass, 2007). Print.

William Byrnes. *Management and the Arts, Fourth Edition* (Oxford: Focal Press, 2009). Print.

Stephen Langly. *Theatre Management and Production in America* (New York: Drama Book Publishers, 1990). Print.

Cheryl Woodward and Lucia Wang. *Every Nonprofit's Guide to Publishing: Creating Newsletters, Magazines & Websites People Will Read* (Berkeley, CA: Nolo, 2007). Print.

APPENDIX

Collaborative Learning Engagement

"The Pitch" Collaborative Learning Engagement

You will be approaching the IMAGE-N Theatre Company with an idea for the season of plays to be produced next year. The Producer has informed you that your team will be given ten to twelve minutes to pitch your idea(s) to the selection committee composed of both employees of the theatre company and its board of directors. Because time is precious, the Producer will stop you once you reach twelve minutes, regardless of whether or not you have finished. Completing the pitch before the ten minute mark will indicate to the group that you are less than prepared.

It is important to the selection committee to hear from each member of the collaborative team. It is also important that the paperwork turned in to the Producer for further consideration clearly highlights your choices, vision, and unique take on the chosen piece. This paperwork should be generated on standard sized paper and turned over to the selection committee in an accordian file folder after your pitch is made.

If the team would like to generate this material and present it to the committee digitally (via *Moodle*, *Dropbox*, or a *Google* site), then please consult the Producer. There will be a short question session following the pitch. This will be led by the Producer.

DIRECTOR

Determine an initial Vision & Concept for your production. This may be revised or reworded at early stages of collaboration.

At the first official production meeting with your group (the production team), guide them through the production intention, and communicate a key moment of the play in terms of your initial Vision & Concept. Remember, this is an exercise in collaboration, so:

Encourage input from all the members of your group. Make sure to keep everyone on task and focused on the unity of production. Be sure to nurture the talents and choices from your group.

To be handed in:

- ▶ Write a one- to three-page, word processed paper explaining your final Directorial Vision & Concept.

- ▶ Using all of this information as a beginning place, choose a key moment in the play and block it using appropriate stage directions (Upstage, Downstage, Center, etc.). Additionally, consider using this scene as the guiding moment for "pitching" your production.

- ▶ What is your directorial Vision & Concept? Make sure to include a statement of theme(s); the style of production to be used. Why is the style appropriate, and what type of theatre space you will be utilizing?

- ▶ How will these choices manifest themselves on stage?

- ▶ How will the design elements fit into this production? How will they serve the Vision & Concept?

- ▶ Using all of this information as a beginning place, choose a key moment in the play and block it using appropriate stage directions.

DRAMATURG

Consult with your director and group to find areas where you could enhance their comprehension of the play. Research appropriate topics accordingly.

Use any and all resources at your disposal: books, trade journals, the internet, your instructor, etc. Remember that the web is a great starting point, but be wary of what you find online. Make sure to check the information against more traditional sources.

You are the collector of information. If the designers have visuals they want to use for the "pitch," then perhaps consider holding them until the appropriate time.

To be handed in:

- ▶ A research bibliography in proper MLA format. There should be more books, articles, etc. than web sources.

- ▶ Information about playwright, production history, and other pertinent facts that might be useful to your production.

- ▶ A two-paragraph summary of the play that would serve as the basis for program notes and the press release.

- ▶ Sample Glossary of Terms from the play.

- ▶ A written description of what will be included in the lobby— both the information that will be presented and any display you feel will help ready the audience for the production.

SCENIC DESIGNER

Consult with your group and director.

Identify your design concept. Remember to adhere to the directorial Vision & Concept while making your own choices.

Locate and research visuals that might inspire your design.

Follow the design process.

To be handed in:

- ▶ Detailed ground plan of scenery, furniture, and the like.
- ▶ Color rendering of set and/or set model.
- ▶ Visual inspiration and/or collage.
- ▶ List of locations and time of day for each scene (Scene Breakdown).
- ▶ A one-page explanation as to why this design "works" with the directorial Vision & Concept.

COSTUME DESIGNER

Consult with your director and group.

Adhere to the directorial Vision & Concept while making your own choices.

Locate and research visuals that might inspire your design.

Write a description of each costume, listed by character.

Follow the design process.

To be handed in:

- ▶ Initial thumbnail sketches of at least four costumes.

- ▶ Two complete color renderings of a final design. You may trace the clothing or perhaps even use clippings from magazines. You may want to consider adding fabric swatches to the final rendering.

- ▶ Visual inspiration and/or collage.

- ▶ A one-page explanation as to why this design "works" with the directorial Vision & Concept.

LIGHTING DESIGNER

Consult with the members of your group and the director. Be sure your lighting enhances the other design elements and does not alter color or texture, etc.

Adhere to the director's Vision & Concept, but make your own choices. Follow the design process.

Fill out the lighting cue chart for the key moment as decided in consultation with your director.

Consider each shift in mood. Consider colors. Consider how to integrate projections into your design.

Make sure to use the information provided in your script to guide your choices.

To be handed in:

► Lighting Cue sheets for the "key moment" scene—completely filled out in detail.

► A one-page discussion of your intention and approach to your design while explicating how it supports and enhances the directorial Vision & Concept.

► A list of slides, projections, or other "special effects" to be used.

► Examples of visual inspiration.

SOUND DESIGNER

Consult with the members of your group and the director.

Adhere to the director's Vision & Concept, but make your own choices.

Fill out the sound cue chart for the "key moment" as decided by your director.

Consider each shift in mood. Consider time period. Consider style of production.

Make sure to use the information provided in the script. Are there natural sounds? Will the production be underscored with music? Are there practical sounds?

To be handed in:

▶ Sound Cue sheets for the "key moment" completely filled out in detail.

▶ A one-page discussion of your intention and approach to your design and how it supports and enhances the directorial Vision & Concept.

▶ A list of sound effects both musical and otherwise, i.e. phone ringing, birds chirping, underscoring, etc.

▶ You may make a recording if you like.

PUBLIC RELATIONS

Consult with your group during initial collaboration.

Gather pertinent information from each person on the production team that can and will be funneled into your press campaign.

Draft a press release.

Design a logo for this production.

Design the program cover or poster.

Continue to consult with the production staff as the ideas they have might shift.

To be handed in:

- ▸ Final press release (typed in proper format).

- ▸ Logo for the production (color, ink or computer generated).

- ▸ Program cover or poster (color, ink or computer generated).

- ▸ A one-page marketing/advertising plan for how you will "sell" this show (consider your audience and how best to get information to them. Be sure to include a "target audience.").

Index of Terms

Index of Exercises